The Experts

Jim Gilbert — a salmon fishing guide at age 13 and one of the coast's "top rods" reveals the pro's secrets for finding salmon and how to catch them using driftfishing techniques and skills. He provides a step-by-step introduction to driftfishing. **Doug Field** — fisherman, guide and lure manufacturer explains the intricacies of successfully fishing the famous Buzz-Bomb. Most fishermen misuse this lure — get it right from the man who heads the Buzz-Bomb Lure Corporation. **Bob Straith** — "top rod" and fishing gear wholesaler knows his lures. He explains in detail how to use the Stingsilda to best advantage, including information on how to modify this already successful lure to meet specific needs. **"Tats" Gatley** — the man behind the well-known Deadly Dick provides inside information on these lures, which color to use at what depth, how to spin cast and much more — a real insider's look. **Dave Stewart** — fishing author and one of our top pros, fills you in on the Rip Tide, Striker and Laser and the secrets behind their successful use. Learn how Dave limits out time and again with these lures. **Charlie White** — author of many best-selling fishing books reveals the clues which tip top fishermen to the location of bait fish and feeding salmon. His background information on salmon is a must read for fishermen. **Lee Straight** — long-time outdoors editor and well-known fisherman provides a step-by-step to the ins and outs of mooching. He explains what most fishermen do wrong and how to do it right. **Ted Peck** — charter fishing guide, ex-broadcaster and light tackle expert, provides a revealing look at the life and habits of chinook and coho salmon and how to use those habits to the fisherman's advantage.

DRIFTFISHING

by Jim Gilbert et al

Illustrations By Nelson Dewey

A Division of
Maclean Hunter

Special Interest Publications

CONTENTS

PART THREE
EXPERT ADVICE ON FISH AND FISHING

Photo credits: photos pages 38, 44, 78 and 150 by Penny McDonald

PART ONE

Driftfishing Fundamentals

By Jim Gilbert

JIM GILBERT

Jim Gilbert, the author of Part One of this book, was born and raised at Brentwood Bay on southern Vancouver Island. In 1927 his father, the late Harry Gilbert, founded a sports fishing marina which is still in operation today under the family name.

At the age of 13, Jim was guiding salmon fishermen on Saanich Inlet – a profession he pursued for some 30 years, attaining recognition as one of Western Canada's finest professional salmon fishing guides.

Today he runs a firm which imports and manufactures fishing lures. He is an appointed member of both the Sports Fish Advisory Board and the Fisheries and Oceans Research Council. He is also a director of the Sports Fishing Institute of B.C. and for the past 20 years has taught a self-designed course covering all aspects of saltwater angling.

Jim is also a recognized and successful artist who teaches and works primarily in a graphic and sculptural form based on the style of the Northwest Coast Indians. His works may be found in collections locally and abroad.

Jim lectures and writes extensively on sportfishing and currently writes a monthly column for a Victoria magazine.

When time permits, Jim enjoys his first love, sportfishing, preferring light-tackle angling for salmon and bottom fish while inventing and testing lures and perfecting sportfishing techniques.

INTRODUCTION

As enthusiasm for saltwater sportfishing continues to grow along the Pacific Coast, driftfishing becomes increasingly popular. "Driftfishing" implies fishing from a drifting boat, which is what the majority of driftfishermen do. Other anglers use the same or similar methods while fishing from anchored boats or from shores, docks and breakwaters.

No one name seems totally and uniquely to describe all the variations and techniques used in this type of angling. It is not unlike the centuries-old method of handline jigging for bottomfish with a heavy, hook-festooned jig. All we have done is changed our tackle to a lighter lure and fished it on a rod and reel.

Today, Pacific driftfishing entails fishing with a painted or plated metal, rapidly-sinking lure, weighing from one-half to four ounces and varying from about two to six inches in length. It is a lure fastened alone to the line (without weights, "hardware," etc.) which gets its action generally through alternately lifting and lowering the rod tip.

All we have done to improve the primitive method of handline "jiggin'" is to attach new, lightweight (18 to 200 gram) lures to monofilament lines on lightweight modern fishing rods and employ different techniques. We have developed "sonic" shaped lures with refined colors, finishes and strong, alloyed steel hooks. As a result, most lures have a quick, erratic, fluttering and tumbling "sonic" action as they fall free on a slack line, a line seldom heavier than 20-pound-test.

This is a light tackle fishery! With only a lure on the line, we are able to fish with sporting gear from the surface down to depths exceeding 100 feet. We need little paraphernalia — only a rod, reel, line and lure — and often the least expensive at that. Yet, with this basic outfit, even the novice fisherman can quickly learn to take fish consistently at any time of year.

Driftfishing really reduces angling to its basics. Although pioneered in Vancouver Island waters in the early '60s, it has proven productive wherever large fish, such as salmon, trout, bass, rockfish and tuna feed on smaller fish.

Since one does not require an engine and can angle in quiet solitude with basic lightweight rod and reel, line and lure, I predict driftfishing is here to stay. It will grow in popularity and attract an ever-increasing following not only along our Pacific Coast, but anywhere anglers chase big fish which naturally chase little fish.

"Good luck and good fishing!"

Jim Gilbert
Vancouver Island, B.C.

CHAPTER 1

BASIC
SKILLS

The most consistent thing about fishing is its inconsistency. For example, many theories and resultant techniques which catch fish today can result in a skunk tomorrow and have to be re-thought or abandoned. The responses of fish to various fishing techniques, methods and lures are not always known. We only theorize, and our theories are often proven wrong. But isn't this what makes fishing enjoyable and challenging?

A good fisherman should have a thorough knowledge of basic skills and techniques. He should know where and when to vary and change these techniques; he should know his tackle, fishing areas and methods, and be able to "read" the water and "know his fish": its basic biology and environment.

Statistics show that 50 per cent of sports-caught salmon on the B.C. coast are taken by only five per cent of the fishermen! Most of these "five per cent top-rods" feel "basic luck" plays only a minor role in their success.

Most novice anglers disagree. They have lots of luck, most of it bad! In any given licence year, 50 per cent of all salmon anglers in B.C. do not catch even one salmon.

However, this situation can be changed using the information contained in this book. If applied, it should make the difference between *fishing* and *catching*.

Today's angler is competing for a generally declining resource and there can be a great deal of empty water between fish. Therefore, anglers who wish to be more successful must astutely observe, listen and constantly learn and acquire new information, facts, skills, techniques and tackles.

THE APPEAL OF DRIFTFISHING

Driftfishing is appealing because the light tackle is hand-held (rather than secured in a boat's rod holder) and the use of ''sporty'' outfits permits maximum play and sport from your fish as you set the hook.

When driftfishing you are constantly holding and working your rod; you can feel the thrill of the strike and see the pull and strain of the fish. Driftfishing is enjoyable and satisfying in the sense that it is a quiet, relaxing type of fishing which does not require a noisy, smelly engine. However, when practised as suggested, it *will* produce fish.

Driftfishing is a conservation-oriented, environmental fishery: You consume no gasoline, create no noise and can relax and have a close association with nature. You can hear and see all manner of creatures below, on, and above the water. It is an excellent type of fishery to be conducted from a rowboat or even a kayak or canoe — where you get exercise plus fish!

For those who have no access to a boat, this method of angling permits the opportunity to catch fish while angling from a permanent shore platform such as a wharf or breakwater.

FAMILY PARTICIPATION

Everyone in the family can participate in this fishery. Even Junior, as long as he can ''work'' a rod up and down. Indeed, younger fishermen with small, unsophisticated outfits (even handlines) often catch just as many fish as Dad with all his ''hotshot'' gear. A number of lures can be fished from a boat, and even four lines from a 15-footer is not uncommon. Remember, just keep the rods spread apart as far as possible and stagger line depths to prevent tangling.

This fishery is effective for salmon even in dogfish-infested waters. It enables you to fish and yet remain fairly dogfish-free since these small sharks will not take a driftfish lure as readily as baited lures.

CHAPTER 2

DRIFTFISHING GEAR

Your rod and reel should be balanced and fairly light since you will be holding and working it constantly. After two or three hours of fishing, even the lightest outfit feels as if it weighs 100 pounds. Rods which have produced best over a long period are lightweight, hollow glass models from seven to 10 feet in length. Most lightweight, non-corrosive reels, especially ocean-type spinning reels, are suitable for driftfishing.

RODS

Rods should have a comfortable foregrip, noncorrosive hardware and good quality tip and guides to permit free movement of your line and a small swivel. Recommended rods for salmon are ocean-spinning or mooching types with medium tip action.

"Highliner" driftfishermen often have two outfits. One is usually a 10-11 foot model (with a soft limber tip action) which is used when fishing shallow waters (surface to 35 feet). When lifted it does not produce an exaggerated, abrupt, or excessively lengthy lift to the lure. For deeper waters (35 feet or more), a rod of seven to nine feet with a medium limber tip is used. This somewhat stiffer tip permits a quicker line lift to activate your lure.

You also need some degree of tip stiffness under long-line conditions to set the hook when you "strike up." On long-lines there is considerable stretch in the monofilament. Line stretch, together

When considering driftfishing gear, think light. Short rod butts are easier to work when driftfishing.

with soft-tipped rods, can result in insufficient lure movement or "pull" when you "strike" and set the hook.

Generally speaking, money spent on better, perhaps costlier, rods is money well spent. Cheaper rods often have poorer quality glass blanks, hardware, wrapping and finish.

REELS

Many, if not most, lightweight reels adapt themselves to this fishery. They should be naturally noncorrosive, light, have sufficient line capacity and be well lubricated. Many fishermen use ocean-type spinning reels. These are probably the most versatile. Some use single-action, multiplier, star-drag, level-wind casting, side casting or lateral reels.

When choosing a reel, keep the weight factor in mind. The lighter the better, but don't sacrifice durability and strength for line capacity. Look also for a dependable, adjustable drag or tension-nut system and an audible ratchet setup. Your reel should have a line capacity of at least 300 yards in order to cope with those particularly energetic salmon which take long runs. I prefer a light, five-inch, single-action reel, loaded with 1,000 feet of 20-pound-test line. With this line and reel I am very versatile: I can cast (by

A typical saltwater spinning reel.

stripping line off the reel onto the boat floor) to fish the surface horizontally, or, by permitting my cast-out lure to sink, I can retrieve it any any angle or depth I desire. But generally, casting or spinning out a lure is best done with a spinning or side-cast reel.

A mooching reel can be adapted to strip casting.

When fishing with a single-action reel (Daiwa 175, 275, or Zebco Z300), I simply strip line off and drop my line vertically while counting the number of line ''pull outs'' so that I know my depth.

To strip line out by this method, hold the rod at foregrip with your left hand and pull line off the reel with your right hand — usually down and away from the reel in pulls which approximate two feet in length. Then let go, permitting the extracted line to slip out through the guides. Repeat the procedure by moving the right hand back up and taking the line at the reel again.

LINE, LEADERS AND SWIVELS

Monofilament lines, either nylon or perlon, which have little stretch lend themselves best to this type of fishing. Low, lineal stretch qualities in line permit a more direct and responsive transfer of rod action to activate your lure and instant "strike pull" to set the hook. Color of line is of little importance.

Lines in excess of 20-pound-test are generally not necessary. Lines in the 12 to 15-pound-test range allow you to put more on the reel. They also permit you to achieve longer distances when spinning or casting. Lines of lighter test have less diameter and bulk, and thus do not have the buoyancy or frictional resistance to the water or its currents. Consequently, a lure on lighter test lines will sink faster and remain at greater depths even in moving water or from a moving boat.

The lure-end portion of line gets a lot of movement and surface wear and is susceptible to abrasions and possible nicks and cuts. A good habit is to cut and discard about 30 feet of your line every dozen or so fishing trips. Discard this line in the ship's garbage, not overboard. Monofilament line floats and discarded line can become tangled in a sea bird's feet and wings, or ball up tight around a propellor.

There are a lot of pros and cons to the use of leaders with driftfish lures. Many successful fishermen tie lures directly onto their line, particularly lures through which the leader or line passes, such as the Buzz-Bomb. Leaders are usually of lighter test strength than the main line. It is generally agreed that when fishing spooky, gear-shy fish in crystal clear water, lighter leaders make for more strikes. Smaller diameter test leaders are less visible, show less of a silhouette against the water's surface, and permit a much freer, more appealing action to the lure as it sinks.

Depending on conditions, size of salmon, rod, lure and depth. I use leaders of 12 to 15-pound-test when using driftfish lures in the 20 to 40 gram size. My leaders are fastened to my main line with a small swivel (crane-type Number 3, 4 or 5; ballbearing size Number 1 or 2; or beadchain Number 20 or 61).

When fishing surface coho or chinook up to and including fish in the 15-pound range, I use the smaller swivel (less visible and bulky) and leaders in the 12 to 15-pound-test range. The larger and deeper

EYE-CROSSER KNOT

gives 100% knot strength

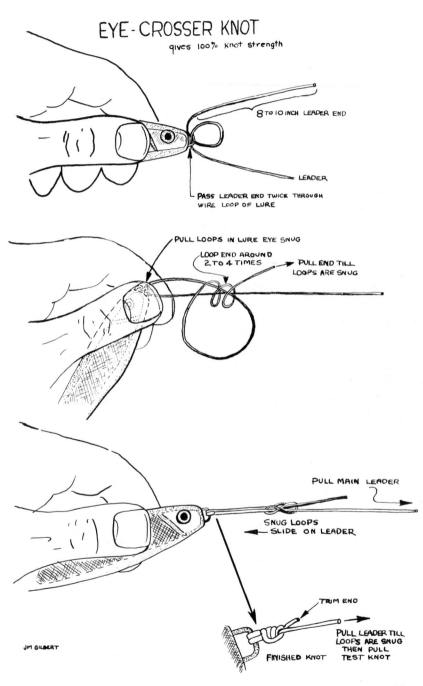

8 TO 10 INCH LEADER END

LEADER

PASS LEADER END TWICE THROUGH WIRE LOOP OF LURE

PULL LOOPS IN LURE EYE SNUG

LOOP END AROUND 2 TO 4 TIMES

PULL END TILL LOOPS ARE SNUG

PULL MAIN LEADER

SNUG LOOPS SLIDE ON LEADER

JIM GILBERT

TRIM END

FINISHED KNOT

PULL LEADER TILL LOOPS ARE SNUG THEN PULL TEST KNOT

19

the salmon, the heavier the leader I use — in some cases in the 18 to 20-pound-test range. When fishing bottomfish (halibut, cod, snapper) use at least 25 to 30-pound-test leader.

Some driftfish lures revolve and twist as they sink, depending on their shape. Some actually spiral when retrieved. Fastening these lures directly to the main line can cause line-twist. However, this will not occur if a swivel is used when joining your leader to the main line.

Leader lengths should never exceed rod lengths. This means that with rod tip held up, you can net your fish without having to pass the swivel through rod tip or guides. A swivel passing over or out through guides or tip can sometimes result in enough resistance to pop a light-test leader. Terminal line twist can also occur while "playing" a hooked and revolving salmon.

Blueback and coho twist and roll a great deal when they're fighting. It's at this time that a swivel permits circular or spiral movement of your terminal leader only and not the main line. Also, some fishermen employ a leader swivel as a "line-up" indicator. When retrieving your line at dawn or dusk the "click" of the swivel indicates that your lure is up. Practical leader lengths have been found to be half to two-thirds of a rod length.

Check your leader and knot for teeth cuts and nicks at the lure end, and "pull-test" the leader at the knot after each fish. After any fish whose poundage approximates or exceeds the test-weight of your leader, discard a few terminal inches and re-tie the knot. The teeth of a fish can nick or cut the leader.

If the leader becomes wrapped around the hook during a struggle, the sharp, barbed slice of the hook can cut as well. I generally change my entire leader after each fishing trip, especially when using lighter tests.

One of the most common mistakes people make is applying a snap-swivel or quick-change arrangement on which to fasten your lure. Always tie your leader *directly* to the lure. A snap-type swivel can seriously upset the action of a lure and make it "fishably" unacceptable. Some fishermen tie their leader to a small splitring at the eye-end of the lure, opposite the hook. With some lures this permits freer, more erratic movement. Use extra-strong, stainless or brass rings (Size 4 or 5) and soft-solder ring joints before tying on your leader. Just touch the wire end of the joints of the ring with a coating of soft-solder to make it much stronger and to prevent accidental opening. I recommend that you do this with all brass splitrings, especially those which hold the hook. With a weighted lure of this type and size, it is extremely easy for a fighting fish to twist open any splitring. The time spent soft-soldering brass splitrings on all driftfish lures is time well spent and in the course of a season will result in many more fish in the boat.

There are many good knots for monofilament material. One of the best I have found for tying all gear, whether it be swivels, lure or hook, is the "eye-crosser" knot.

This knot, if tied correctly, will result in a knot of almost 100 per cent line strength, whereas most knots are only good for up to 80 or 90 per cent of line strength. When tying any knot in monofilament material, always work with an adequate end, and wet your material for minimum surface abrasion when pulling the knot tight.

Pull the knot loops or wraps down slowly and with a steady strain. Pull-test all knots after tying; even the finest looking knots in monofilament material will inexplicably break loose. It is better to have a knot break in your hand than in the fish's mouth 50 feet away.

Lures which are 60 g and heavier can cause knot-leader fatigue at the point where the line wraps tight around the fastening eye of the lure. Fatigue of monofilament line results when subjected to continual jerk-strains as the lure works on the end of the leader. It is good practice to check your knot strength with an even, steady hand-pull every 15 minutes or so, especially with the heavier lures.

HOOKS THAT 'HOOK'

Salmon skin is extremely tough. A hook only barely embedded in a strip of skin is sufficient to hold through a struggle to the net. But salmon scales and skin are difficult to penetrate with a hook point, and only an extremely sharp hook will take, enter and hold. Hooks on driftfish lures should be "grabby" or "sticky." All points should be honed or filed needle-sharp so they will "grab" and hold the fish no matter where they hit. "Toprods" sharpen all hooks every time out, and particularly after touching or 'snagging' bottom.

Test the sharpness of the hook on your fingernail. Drag the point at 90 degrees to the nail surface. If it doesn't dig in and scratch the nail, keep sharpening until it does.

I do not feel that the color of the hook is very important but the strength and size is crucial. Always replace rusty hooks with others of identical size and weight. Changing hooks and sizes can change the lure's action. Smaller hooks can make for more lure action; larger hooks are heavier and may result in less lure action. I

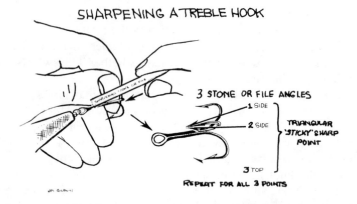

SHARPENING A TREBLE HOOK

3 STONE OR FILE ANGLES

1 SIDE
2 SIDE
3 TOP

TRIANGULAR 'STICKY' SHARP POINT

REPEAT FOR ALL 3 POINTS

have found single hooks of the "siwash" type (found on trolling spoons) hook and hold extremely well on all driftfish lures. Replacement single hooks should always be of a weight similar to the removed treble hook. The single hook is placed so that the hook points face in towards the concave side of 'C' bent lures.

CHAPTER 3

DRIFTFISHING LURES

There are many driftfish lures available today. Some of the most popular are the Buzz-Bomb, Norwegian and Canadian "Sildas," Danish Pirken, the Deadly Dick and the Riptide Strikes. These are available in a range of sizes from two to six inches and weights ranging from five to 125 g and larger. They are also available in a number of colors and plated finishes. The most important features of any lure are:

• Lure action
• Method and techniques of fishing the lure
• Area and depth to be fished
• Lure size
• Lure color

LURE ACTION

A lure's action depends on a number of factors. These include shape, weight, size, balance and hooking arrangement. Productive driftfish lures are those whose shapes match those of the bait fish. When coupled with this natural bait fish shape, lures can have built-in structural angles, contours and edges which produce actions and possible vibrations which represent the action of a wounded bait fish. When you've created this you have a lure which will be a fish-catcher.

The action of the lure is one of the most important factors in this fishery. To reach its peak of *fishability*, a lure must work right and always "sound right." A salmon's eyesight is not great and I am sure that vibrations can always be picked up before it sees a lure. Therefore it is often attracted to the vicinity of a lure by sound;

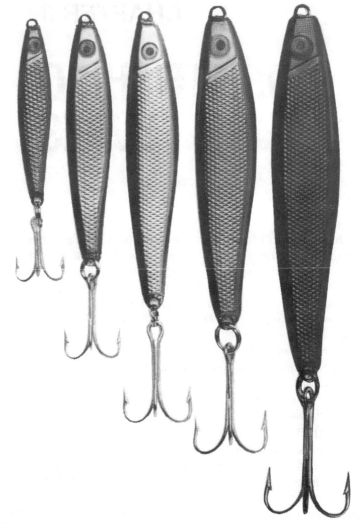

The Jensen Pirks, shown here in the 7 to 40 g sizes, are the author's favorite driftfishing lures. Customized bending of the Pirk is not recommended.

then it strikes the lure, possibly because its action is associated with the natural movements of a wounded bait fish.

Feeding salmon strike many lures as a result of a conditioned response mechanism. This response is greatest at times of activity and feeding by the salmon. There must be a great deal of frenzied feeding activity taking place in the summer and fall months for salmon to grow as much as a pound per week.

Salmon are predators. They are extremely aggressive and competitive when feeding is taking place, and fussy when the "bite" is over and their stomachs are full.

It is difficult to describe the action of the lure which produces best in the greatest number of areas and under the greatest number of conditions. When fishing an area where salmon are naturally feeding on herring minnows or anchovy, the lure action which succeeds in the majority of situations is best described as having an erratic, horizontal, sideways-fluttering, horizontally-revolving or spinning action. On its way down, a lure should dart out and down at irregular angles. The complete range of these actions is obtainable only by permitting the lure to sink free on slack line. The majority of fish will strike it on the free-slack, sinking stroke. When driftfishing, the rod's action is a slow, taut up-stroke and a quick, slack down-stroke.

On the up-stroke the lure rises forward or toward you, in a spiral or wobble action. At times this action will produce fish but most often salmon strike on the down-stroke.

I have seen coho vary from day to day and even hour to hour on the type of lure action they prefer. The type, size, movement, concentration and depth of feed change their patterns as does the influence of tide and weather.

Generally, mature, near-spawning coho prefer a dark colored lure with a quick, horizontally-tumbling spinning action. Feeding coho generally prefer a lure with a quicker action than do feeding chinook. At times big chinook appear to be lazy and prefer a slower-acting lure; often they will hit the lure only at the near-stationary end of the down-stroke — often this hit will just be a "mouthing" of the lure. You must strike one of these mouthing fish quick and hard in order to set the hook. A "mouthing fish" can often only be detected by the fact your slack line ceases to sink.

Often when salmon are active "on a bite" they will take just about any action. I've caught chinook salmon on a dead-still lure at the end of a line that was unattended and stationary — even on a lure as it lay motionless on the bottom. Generally speaking, smaller, immature salmon are not nearly as fussy about a lure's action and method of presentation as larger ones.

You can consider a lure to have better than average fish-catching

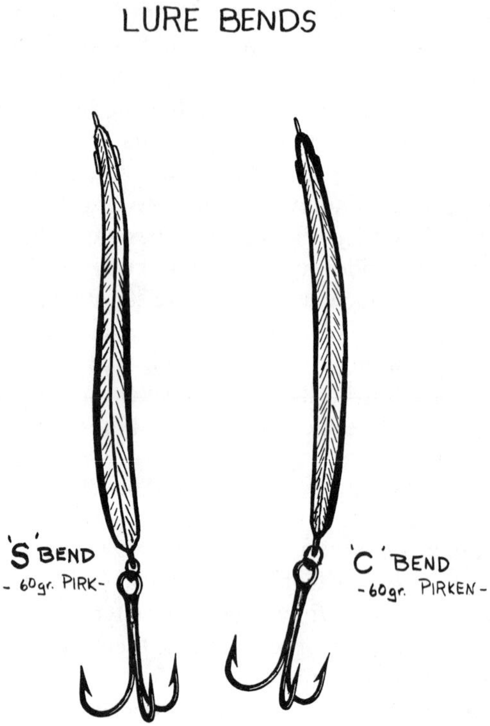

LURE BENDS

'S' BEND
- 60gr. PIRK-

'C' BEND
-60gr. PIRKEN-

action if it will produce a fish when the bite is over and the fish are "off."

There are various ways to successfully change the action of a lure. One, as mentioned earlier, is the addition of a small splitring. This is an alteration which will permit a different and more erratic action on some Sildas and Pirkens. My advice is to use small, nickeled brass splitrings, possibly size Number 3. Just touch the wire end joints of the ring with a coating of soft-solder to make it stronger and prevent opening.

Most highliners favor some customization in the shape, bend, hook, size and/or color of their lure. Generally speaking, minor modifying bends are placed through the back longitudinal axis of some lures.

The bend or shape necessary for sonic vibrations and general fish-catching action is built right into the better lures at the time of manufacture. However some changes in the shape or hook size of any lure will result in a slightly different action. All the same, whether or not this customization will produce fish is a matter of trial and error on the part of the fisherman.

In areas with a great number of variances in tidal conditions, bait fish, salmon sizes and species, you will find the fast, fluttering, horizontal sinking action resulting from the "C" bend in Silda and Pirken lures to be the most productive. This is particularly true when fishing a lure in schools of herring minnow or anchovy.

This "C" bend will produce more action when one is fishing from a drifting boat and working a vertical or near vertical line.

The "S" bend has proved to be outstanding when *trolling* a driftfish lure or when fishing exclusively horizontally (or nearly horizontally).

"S" bends are productive in most areas when spinning or casting. Over the past few years tests have shown that fast-fluttering "C" bend lures may not produce salmon that are feeding on sand lance. Salmon which are feeding on sand lance seem to prefer an elongated lure with a slight "C" or "S" bend which darts erratically as it drops vertically on slack line.

BENDING A LURE

When bending your metal driftfish lures, simply grip the lure with thumb on top, then place thumb of other hand over first thumb and press firmly down on the lure. This should be done with the lure resting on a firm, non-slip surface.

Caution should be exercised in bending plated or hard-coated lures. Cracking the surface can result in peeling and subsequent loss of color and finish.

LURE COLOR

Lure color is probably the most controversial and widely discussed subject among local sportfishermen. After 35 years in the salmon sports fishery, I believe that it is not a major factor in inshore waters. In offshore waters, with changing water colors and feed conditions, color *can* play a great part in success. In protected inshore waters, however, where three- to five-inch bait fish make up the abundance of feed, it is not clearly evident that driftfish lure color is important. Generally, the deeper you fish a lure, the less light is available, therefore the less color there is visible.

In deep water or on dull days, plated lures or lures that have attached metallic film (in the form of a narrow strip along each side) will sometimes produce more fish than painted lures. I have tested all colors — iridescent light strips, fluorescent, luminescent glow paint, even solid black — and they have all caught fish. Colors that I felt were the most consistent over the long haul were those which for the most part truly represented a bait fish's natural color: That is, those lures which had a colored back and silver sides as found on natural bait fish. Color is not nearly as important as the lure's action, method of fishing, depth and area fished. Rather than changing color, try changing your depth, area or technique. To your surprise you may find this will work.

LURES — A CLOSER LOOK

Generally speaking, production driftfish lures "work" on a vertical rather than a horizontal axis, whereas trolled, spun, or casting lures and baits are usually moved along on a horizontal plane. The heavier driftfish lures will sink quite fast when given slack line. Therefore, these lures *must* be given slack lines on which to "work."

Your rod tip should be *pulled* (not jerked) up and permitted to drop quickly down or back so the lure is given that free-falling, slack line on which to "work."

When falling on slack line, a "C" bent lure is extremely erratic in action. And an erratic action is one of the most important features in the "catchability" of any lure. This type of lure has been used for many years in Europe and eastern U.S. waters. It has been perfected and used almost exclusively by Scandinavian and European fishermen in rivers and coastal waters where they take all manner of fish species.

Not until some 30 years ago was this fishing method tried, proven and accepted by salmon anglers on Vancouver Island. Even today many salmon fishermen, especially trollers, have a hard time believing that a salmon will take a "hunk of lead" in preference to herring bait. But I know at times they will!

The vertical movement of the rod tip and line causes the lure to wobble or spiral as it is lifted and to gyrate erratically as it drops. The fish generally take the lure as it sinks free on slack line. In most cases you are not aware of the fish taking the lure until you pull in

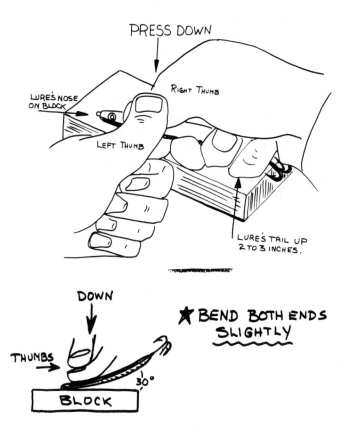

the slack by lifting your rod. When feeling even the slightest strain or resistance you should always strike immediately. There are exceptions. When a fish takes hold on an "up-pull" there is no mistaking a hit. You'll know about it.

Over the course of a season, don't expect an exclusive catch of large salmon with these lures. Driftfish lures are not a "hot" year-round producer. There never has been a fish lure, or method of angling, which will take fish consistently. There are too many variables involved. Driftfishing works best when conducted in association with schools of bait fish or salmon. Trolling will generally outfish driftfish methods when bait fish schools are lacking or when salmon populations are exceptionally deep and dispersed.

THE AUTHOR'S CHOICE

Improvements are constantly being made in driftfishing lures. Some driftfish lures new to the Canadian market are the Danish Jensen Pirk and Pirken. These lures are among the most productive and popular jig-type lures used in Europe. I have helped customize these lures for West Coast waters and can say that Jensen lures are high quality. Pirken have bendable metal alloy, a flexible non-tracking clear finish, and strong treble hooks attached with stainless steel rings. The Pirken comes with a built-in "C" bend and the nickelplated Pirk has a built-in "S" bend. Customized bending of the Pirk is not recommended since the surface nickel plating could crack and peel. The Pirk and Pirken give off sonic vibrations and their balance helps alleviate hook and leader tangles.

CHAPTER 4

FISHING DRIFTFISH LURES

I am not going to advocate the best method to driftfish — there isn't one. There are probably as many methods of working a lure as there are areas in which to fish. Methods and techniques vary according to the time of day, season, year, stage of a salmon's maturity, size and concentration of fish, depth of water, type of bottom, size of bait and tide and current conditions. No lure of any one size, action or color will catch fish consistently. Lures should be changed to match the size and type of bait fish in an area.

A weighted driftfish lure is generally fished using one of four methods or techniques:

- Spinning
- Casting
- Driftfish "jigging" (Not to be confused with snagging)
- Trolling

When using any of these methods the most important detail is that the lure be pulled ahead or up in the water and generally be permitted to sink back freely on slack line.

The majority of fishermen fish a driftfish lure on a saltwater spinning outfit. They cast the lure out from a boat, shore, dock or pier, permit the lure to sink, then retrieve it with alternate "pull up" rod strokes, winding in on the slack or "down-rod" strokes. When you retrieve the lure using this technique, vary the lure

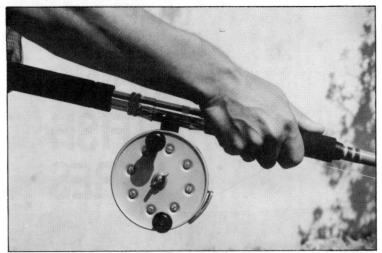

Most fishermen activate their rods too much. Keep rod action to a minimum. The angle of the rod at the bottom of the down stroke is shown above; angle at the top of the up stroke is shown below.

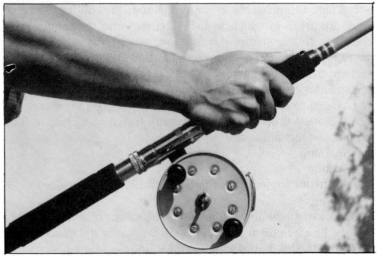

retrieval actions — speed up or slow down — and vary the length of rod-pull strokes from eight to 36 inches.

I believe that the majority of fishermen activate their rods *too much*, indeed so much so that under some circumstances the fish have difficulty in seizing the lure. Rod pulls of five to six feet are usually unproductive and excessive.

Variations are limitless. Vary your lure depth, speed of retrieval, your duration and length of rod pulls, and periodically include the odd hesitation in your retrieval. Occasionally try quick-quick, slow-slow rod pulls, activating the rod tip only six to eight inches. Never let your rod tip get so high during any of the "pull up" strokes that it restricts your hook-setting, striking effort.

COMMON MISTAKES

When working a lure many people mistakenly *jerk* their rod instead of slowly pulling it. A rod pull from 12 inches to four feet is usually all that is necessary. Jerking a stiff-tipped rod will often result in your lure jumping, inverting and doubling the hook over the leader, essentially rendering it "unfishable." This can be detected, however, by abnormal vibrating and resistance when the rod tip is pulled up. To prevent this, pull your rod up without jerking, or try a lighter tipped rod. Remember, when fishing shorter lines, shorter pulls are necessary. However, the deeper you go, the longer you will need to pull because of line stretch.

The greatest mistake you can make in this type of fishery is in not permitting the rod to drop back quickly enough to permit slack line on which the lure can "work." Always watch your sinking line, both when you are letting it out, and on rod "drop-stroke;" if it stops abruptly, wind it in quickly until you feel resistance, then set the hook immediately.

VARY YOUR TECHNIQUE

Vary your technique until you "connect" with a fish, then stay with that combination as long as the fish will take it. Once the feeding depth has been determined, it may be quicker to simply drop your lure off and out from the end of the rod rather than to cast or spin it out and let it sink. When stripping line from your reel always count the number of "strip-offs" so you can duplicate the depth.

When salmon are feeding on sand lance over a hard, clean sand bottom, let your lure hit the seabed, then retrieve it only enough so that your lure will flutter down onto it again.

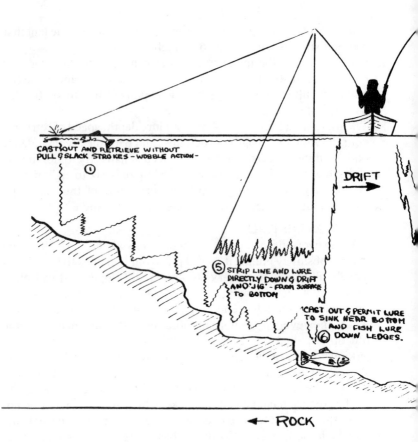

CAST OUT AND RETRIEVE WITHOUT
PULL & SLACK STROKES — WOBBLE ACTION —
①

DRIFT →

⑤ STRIP LINE AND LURE
DIRECTLY DOWN & DRIFT
AND 'JIG' — FROM SURFACE
TO BOTTOM

CAST OUT & PERMIT LURE
TO SINK NEAR BOTTOM
AND FISH LURE
⑥ DOWN LEDGES.

← ROCK

In any driftfishery remember to fish your lure right to the surface. Even when retrieving your lure for inspection, always "fish" it in. Vary your strokes, speed and duration. Salmon are great followers and will strike at the most unpredictable times. I have seen coho jump out of the water not two feet from a boat in pursuit of a lure that was too quickly retrieved and lifted from the water.

Whenever possible always look into the water and observe your lure as it is retrieved. (Visibility is better in calm, clear water with the sun at your back.) If you see salmon following your lure, slow down and vary your action with short pulls — possibly no more than six to 12 inches. Any lure action change can often "trigger" a salmon to strike, and what a thrill it is to see a salmon hit a lure only a few feet under the water, right beside the boat.

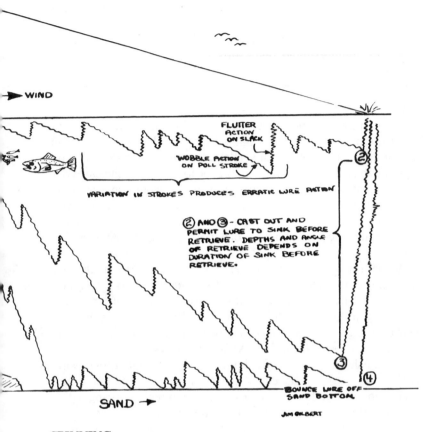

WIND

FLUTTER ACTION ON SLACK

WOBBLE ACTION ON POLL STROKE

VARIATION IN STROKES PRODUCES ERRATIC LURE ACTION

② AND ③ - CAST OUT AND PERMIT LURE TO SINK BEFORE RETRIEVE. DEPTHS AND ANGLE OF RETRIEVE DEPENDS ON DURATION OF SINK BEFORE RETRIEVE.

②

③

④

BOUNCE LURE OFF SAND BOTTOM

SAND →

JIM GILBERT

SPINNING

An ocean-spinning outfit is ideal for driftfishing from shore or boat. In an open boat, a spinning outfit permits you to cover all 360 degrees of surrounding surface area. It also has the advantage of permitting you to drop a lure into shallow water and retrieve it without hitting bottom. Spinning is particularly advantageous when fish are feeding on or near the surface or in shallow water. When you see bait fish "break" the surface or salmon show or "boil" under bait fish, it is relatively easy to place your lure in front of the feeding salmon. More often than not this technique will result in an immediate strike. Limber monofilament lines of 12- to 15-pound-test are best suited for ocean spinning reels because they permit maximum length of casts with minimum foul-ups, twists and tangles.

35

A recent driftfishing technique developed by Saanich Inlet anglers starts out by casting the line as far as possible and letting the lure sink vertically until it hits bottom. Then they retrieve the lure with uninterrupted quick lifts of the rod (two-three feet), followed by fast wind-ins on the down stroke. Excellent results have been achieved, particularly on late summer and fall salmon.

CASTING OPTIONS

Fairly new on the scene and growing in popularity with driftfishermen are the Australian side-cast reels. These reels can be operated as conventional single-action models or swivelled on movable bases (at right angles to the rod axis) so you can cast your line out from a fixed, stationary spool as you would on a spinning reel. Then simply turn your reel on the seat and reel it in as you would a single-action reel. This is an old concept in reel use, but incorporates the better features of a fixed spool and a single-action reel.

As with any single-action reel, you spool the reel with your fingertips only. When "playing" a fish and when it is "running" you exert only a *slight* finger-tip pressure at the bottom of the revolving drum. An amateur or an excited novice fisherman must learn to keep fingers out of the way of handles. This is why single-action reels are called "knuckle-dusters."

Some fishermen cast driftfish lures with a multiplier level-wind reel. This should be fished so that your reel and rod guides are facing up and not down as with single-action reels. Casting with a level-wind reel is not recommended for amateurs since the reels are susceptible to line-tangle and must be thumb-controlled on the cast. Moreover, some models do not lend themselves to the use of monofilament line.

JIGGING

Jigging means simply stripping off line (with an attached lure) straight down from your boat. The line angle, or angle of retrieve, will depend upon the weight of line and lure, how far you let your line out, or how fast your boat or the current is moving. When fishing this method, vary the depths of your lures, trying to determine where the strike zone is; if you do find the strike zone or the area where the fish are feeding on bait fish, then move all your lures to that depth.

Repeated dropping of your lure to the feeding depth can be accomplished by counting the number of strip-outs that you take off your reel. If your boat has a depth sounder, drop your lures to bait mass level or slightly below the school.

Whether the line is coming in or going out, if you feel any bump or hit or have sudden stops on a sinking line, quickly jerk your rod tip and strike.

Salmon will often take hold of a sinking lure and you must strike to set the hook. They often take a free falling line, head for the surface, jump and throw the lure. These salmon are very frustrating to hook and are called "toppers." In order to hook these fish, you must quickly reel in your slack line until you feel tautness or pressure, and then attempt to strike the fish.

Similarly, on retrieve, many salmon will follow and simply bump a lure. If you feel this slight movement, stop, slow your retrieve, and alter your pattern of rod movement. A change in retrieval speed or action will often entice the "playing" fish to strike. Often these bumps are the result of a salmon hitting the lure with its tail or body. A coho, in particular, will slap a lure with its body to stun or cripple before taking the lure in its mouth. This is the reason you periodically hook salmon in the body or tail, in fact, anywhere. This has led to a great deal of adverse publicity for driftfishing. People think driftfishermen are snagging or foul-hook jigging salmon.

TROLLING

Driftfish lures can be productively fished from a trolled boat when fish are on or near the surface. Faster speeds — up to three or four knots — work especially well on coho and blueback. Slightly slower speeds work well on surface feeding chinook. To be successful, the trolling should be done only when you observe surface feeding fish. This technique is often the only way to catch fish during periods of frenzied surface activity. Rather than simply placing the rod in a rod-holder, you will have better success holding the rod and "working it:" that is, slowly pulling it forward and then slowly allowing it to fall back.

The "S" bend produces best and is not prone to hook tangling around the leader. Seventy-five to 100 feet of line is all that is required. On calm, flat days, longer lines possibly should be used. On choppier, wind-agitated waters, shorter lines are called for, especially for summer feeding coho.

Driftfish lures trolled 20 to 30 feet astern in the prop wash will also take cohos. When trolling driftfish lures, generally troll at speeds faster than you would use with conventional trolling gear.

MATCH THE BAIT FISH

Always examine stomach contents for size and species of bait fish. Lure length should approximate bait fish size. In July, lures of 2½ to three inches, and 25-30 g in weight work well. Productive

Matching lure size to the size of bait fish in the water can pay off in a big way as this happy fisherman demonstrates.

mid-summer lures measure three to 3½ inches and weigh 40 g. By fall or winter, 3½ to four-inch, 60-g sizes work, but there are always exceptions.

When fishing an area where the salmon feed fairly exclusively on sand lance, particularly in early spring and summer, the lance will probably be anywhere from four to 10 inches long and the larger, longer lures are best. In some areas in early summer, fish feed on lance, minnow and anchovy due to an overlap of bait fish schools. At this time you might want to use the 60-g size one day, and the 28-g size the next.

When fishing bottom feeding chinook or when salmon are feeding on six-inch and larger anchovies, lures of four to five inches will produce very well. If you are plagued with small fish when driftfishing, try a larger size lure; often the larger lure will produce a larger fish. Smaller salmon too will often frequent shallow waters; larger salmon will be found deeper.

As with the sand lance, squid populations have increased dramatically. Vast schools of squid can appear at any time of the year, usually frequenting deep water (50-100 feet), often right on the bottom.

Driftfishermen have found lures of 60, 80 and 100-g size in white or pearl colorations catch salmon which are feeding on squid. Best lure action is a vertical darting action with no excessive fluttering. Lures should be fished just above the bottom.

Vinyl lures, such as all-white octopus, cuttlefish or squirts, rigged with tandem 2/0 hooks on a short (24-inch) leader with in-head lead inserts will also catch salmon under these conditions.

PLAYING A SALMON

Playing a fish on a driftfish lure is essentially no different from playing it on any other lightweight gear. Generally, you will find that the term "playing a fish" means not *forcing* it in. This is possibly the most common mistake made by fishermen and often results in a broken leader, tackle or a torn out hook.

People who attempt driftfishing with a rod that has too stiff a tip and who insist on "cranking in" a fighting fish will probably lose large numbers of them in the process. After hooking any fish, a rod tip should be held up high, at least at a 45-degree angle to the surface. A rod tip held this way has "give." Let a salmon have its head and let it run if it wants to. A hooked chinook salmon will often sound in deep water. In shallow waters however, you will have some fantastic runs from salmon which are unable to sound. They simply can't go down so they have to go out!

Hooked salmon on the run can obtain fantastic speeds and exert tremendous strain on your gear. Before a salmon "cleans" your reel of line (I've seen some runs of 900 feet) quickly turn your boat and chase the fish. Attempting to slow down or to stop a large salmon in "full flight" is sheer madness — 99.99 per cent of the time a salmon will simply keep on going with your lure and a broken leader dangling from its mouth.

My experience has shown that with a lure of from two to four ounces, a certain amount of tautness in your line is advisable. With a cartwheeling coho or headshaking chinook a taut line to a rod tip held high is the best way to prevent the hook from being shaken out.

Tire your fish out before attempting to net it. And always net it head first. Equip yourself with a large, light yet strong synthetic bag landing net. Lift large salmon into the boat by taking hold of both sides of the net hoop, not the handle because it can break and you could lose everything.

CHAPTER 5

THE ALL-IMPORTANT BAIT FISH

I find that driftfishing works best when you have active, feeding salmon associated with a volume of small bait fish. Salmon are best taken in an area which has concentrations of herring minnows, anchovy, sand lance or squid. Only occasionally will salmon which are feeding exclusively on large bait fish (in particular herring in excess of six inches) be taken on a driftfish lure. Possibly the action of a driftfish lure rapidly tumbling does not truly represent the natural, wounded action of one of these large bait fish and hence salmon are reluctant to strike it.

For best results when fishing salmon that are feeding on sand lance, your lure should be fished near or virtually on the bottom. Sand lance populations appear to be building and extending their range in the lower Strait of Georgia waters, particularly in areas that have sand bottoms. They form a great part of the salmon's diet in many areas, especially in early spring and summer. At times chinook gorge themselves on these lance and thus can only be taken near the bottom where the lance frequent.

Driftfishing in early spring or summer works best in areas where concentrations of sand lance will be found. Often this will be in shallow water, but sometimes in depths up to 90-100 feet.

When fishing salmon which are feeding on minnows and anchovies (generally regarded as surface or midwater bait fish) "fish" your lure in or slightly below the school of bait fish. Smaller salmon are frequently found feeding right in a bait fish mass, while larger salmon are often slightly below, waiting for sinking cripples that the small salmon above have hit and stunned.

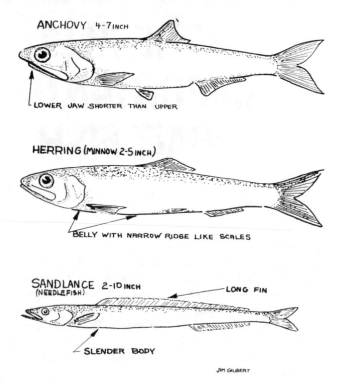

ANCHOVY 4-7 INCH

LOWER JAW SHORTER THAN UPPER

HERRING (MINNOW 2-5 INCH)

BELLY WITH NARROW RIDGE LIKE SCALES

SANDLANCE 2-10 INCH
(NEEDLEFISH)

LONG FIN

SLENDER BODY

JIM GILBERT

In attempting to work out a pattern or timetable for most areas in the Gulf of Georgia, I find that driftfishing for chinook and coho will not hit its peak until large schools of bait fish such as sand lance, anchovy or minnows appear in an area. In many areas this will not occur until the herring spawn hatches, moves from the beach and is recognizable in schools of 2½ to three-inch minnows. This condition is not reached in most areas until June or July. From late June, concentration of shoreline minnows begin to migrate in depths from the surface down to 30 feet.

June and July herring typically frequent inshore, shallow-water areas and the salmon will swim into these areas to feed. When this occurs, shore spinning with driftfish lures will prove effective. As the minnows feed and grow in size (three inches or larger), they will move offshore. By late summer and fall, these little minnows have grown to 4½ to five inches and, by early winter, most have left the inside shore areas with the exception of a few large schools which spend the winter in some of our coastal bays and inlets.

Good fishing can be obtained in areas where winter chinook are feeding on these minnow masses. Remember, however, to fish your lure in, or slightly below, the school of bait fish. These schools can be detected by depth sounder, or by simply observing sea bird activity. Ducks too, feed on bait fish.

ANCHOVY

Anchovy is a bait fish that appears to be increasing its numbers in our coastal waters. Anchovies generally frequent the sounds and inlets of outer Vancouver Island, though they can move into the Strait of Juan de Fuca in early winter. In any area or at any time of year, where you find schools of anchovies, you will find salmon that will take driftfish lures.

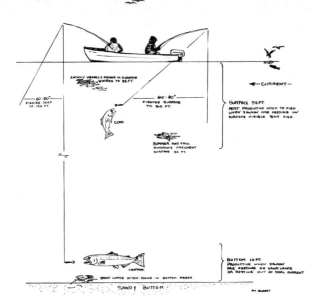

In early summer and fall, driftfishing for chinook in areas on the west coast of Vancouver Island that have resident anchovy populations (Barclay Sound, Nootka, Kyoquot and Quatsino Sound) will frequently yield outstanding results. At these times, be pre-

A double header for these driftfishermen!

pared for large chinook in the 20 to 40 pound range. Seek out areas with anchovy populations. Shore areas with surface-active anchovy schools or "balled up" masses of anchovy are the most productive areas. Gull and diving-duck activity will indicate the location of these schools, then fish directly in and over them. If bait fish schools move, move with them.

To take salmon consistently by driftfishing year-round, without concentrations of feed fish, is no easy feat. Top-rods who can do this, study and know their areas well. They know the tidal current and the fishes' movements and habits. Salmon caught when there is little feed present are usually taken deep and in the majority of cases, are to be found very near the bottom.

SAND LANCE — NEEDLEFISH

Over the past 10 years the sand lance (needlefish) has undergone dramatic increases in abundance and range. Almost every area that was affected by the warming trend of the El Nino current of the early '80s now has large, resident populations of sand lance.

In the winter and spring months, sand lance vary in size from three to eight inches in length and remain in deep water near sand bottoms.

I believe that in times of strong tidal flow, sand lance bury

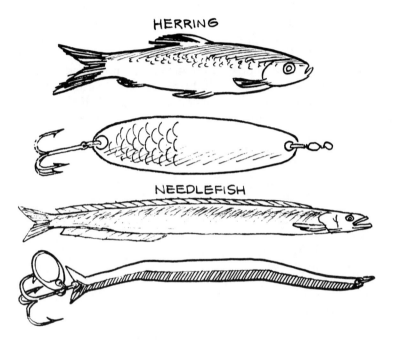

HERRING

NEEDLEFISH

themselves in the sand sub-strata on the bottom. When the tidal current "slackens," these silver, snake-like fish wriggle out and congregate into large compact schools.

At the time of burying or emerging, most sand lance are rendered virtually immobile and vulnerable to all feeding fish. Logically then, driftfish lures should be fished on or near the bottom.

Earlier I mentioned "sonic lures." These are driftfish lures that are said to create vibrations while working in the water. These vibrations or sound waves may be similar to those created by the natural swimming of wounded baitfish. This may be the reason why feeding fish are attracted and possibly why they strike the lure. And in the case of near-spawning, mature fish, this vibration may cause a strike, not because it sounds or looks like a natural feed fish, but because the lure's vibration may simply be an annoyance or aggravation. The vibration, however, is not the only reason that a fish strikes your lure; the lure must also have an action which the salmon associates in some way with that of a natural crippled bait fish.

Sound travels fast through the water. You will find that better results are obtained when driftfishing in shallower waters (down to 25 feet) if you and your boat create as little noise and resultant vibrations as possible. Shut off the motor. Try wearing soft-soled shoes and avoid loud and sharp noises, particularly if your boat is constructed of aluminum. Surface salmon tend to be spooky, especially late, fall-run coho.

CHAPTER 6

THE WHEN & WHERE OF DRIFTFISHING

There is a direct relationship between angling success and populations of fish present in any area. It is not always easy to determine which areas fish frequent. Most amateurs seek "fishy" areas by relying upon the often unproductive theory that if there are a number of fishermen or boats in any area, they must be catching fish. This is not always true. Highliners frequently fish areas which have produced for them in the past, or "read the water" and conditions, and take all factors into consideration. Experience is the key. To help you "read the water" I have included the following information about surface indicators. However this is not complete as after a lifetime of angling I am still learning.

TIDES AND CURRENTS

Tides and currents probably play the biggest role in determining where you will have your greatest success. No fish likes to "buck" a tide flow — bait fish and salmon included. They favor areas of minimal flow such as back-eddies and around points of land or islands. When the tide is flowing bait fish and salmon will often lie in a back-eddy or in a protected stretch out of the main tide flow. If they are migratory salmon, they will often wait until the tide turns and then move at slack water, following contours of the land fairly close to shore.

Rarely do you find concentrations of bait fish without associated

It takes more than luck to make this happen – a good driftfisherman must learn to "read" the water.

salmon. Therefore, watch for surface "flips" in tide areas to see where the currents are meeting. This meeting of the water also moves concentrations of plankton upon which bait fish feed. Success can be achieved by fishing the edge of a tide flow, or in a back-eddy. A lure fished in the main tide flow may look unnatural. Cohos in general feed and swim in back-eddies that form either side of a rip.

Surface swirl and counterswirl may indicate underwater upwelling, usually formed from irregular bottom contours. Such vertical currents are fished in much the same manner as horizontal back eddies. Always fish on the downstream side of an underwater obstruction or point of land. Non-feeding salmon concentrations often lay in these spots. If there is not sufficient tide flow to create vertical currents, seek out surface tide lines (areas where smooth water is abruptly broken into rippled or agitated surface). Areas of little tide flow, off points of land or underwater reefs, will produce better than quiet bays.

Both baitfish and salmon can often be found on the edge of or inside tidelines. These areas also contain much flotsam and jetsam. To prevent line and lure fouling, fish close to the edge rather than in a tideline.

READING THE WATER

Successful fishermen read the water to determine where to fish. They know the tides and their effects on the water; they know whether to fish the flood, change, ebb or intermediate tide state, even when to change positions during the flow. This comes from experience based on observation and study.

There are many surface signs besides tides that may help you determine the area in which to fish. Along with seabirds, the salmon themselves often let you know of their whereabouts; watch for jumpers, rollers or backs just breaking the surface. Note the direction of the jump or roll; this will often indicate the direction in which the fish are moving.

At times salmon will just "fin." Coho, especially, do this, just showing their dorsal fin above the water. Surface-feeding salmon often show as swirls or boils on the water. Fish in pursuit of bait will turn abruptly on or near the surface, leaving telltale dimples or small rings on the surface — often the only sign of bluebacks or coho feeding on larval shrimp.

Bait fish are usually indicated by a "rain drop" effect appearing on the surface. Feeding bait will often break surface — the odd one even jumps. However, don't be fooled by vast amounts of surface activity and jumpers or small fish that you see in May, June and July; they may be young salmon that are ocean bound and fresh from the river.

The ideal salmon fishing situation is when you observe vast areas of bait fish, particularly minnows breaking surface, or complete schools of anchovy "dancing" out of the water. The whole area erupts as bait leaps to escape the pursuit of hungry salmon.

On smooth water, subsurface herring can be found by locating vast areas of minute bubbles, not unlike thousands of square feet of ginger ale effervescence. Minnows and herring release these bubbles from their air bladders as they change depth and the bubbles float to the surface. Some oldtimers can detect schools of underwater herring by scent alone.

During summer and fall months, small herring generally do not swim deeper than 35 feet, usually near shorelines, and feed in

water up-welled by underwater rock outcropping or reefs. However, there are times during the winter when they will go deeper.
Schools of deep bait fish can be found by seeking out deep-diving
ducks such as murres, murrelets, grebes and cormorants.

WATCH THE SEABIRDS

Seabirds and diving ducks are one of the best ways of finding
populations of bait fish. Any time that you see a member of the gull
or tern family on the water, some feed must be about. Investigate

gull or tern activity whenever you see it and you will learn a great
deal. When these birds are actively feeding they cannot keep quiet.
They scream, squawk and carry on very noisily.

Large seabirds such as glaucous-winged and herring gulls are
active in most areas at any time of the year. In winter and spring
they feed on large herring; in spring and summer on lance and
anchovies. Large gulls tend to feed on concentrations of bait fish
where it is easy to consume large amounts in a short time. They
prefer ''ball-ups'' or heavy concentrations of minnows, anchovies,
lance or herring. Small gulls such as Bonapartes, Californias and
terns are usually observed on inshore waters in summer months;
they are usually associated with minnows and sand lance.

Active, screaming gulls and terns swooping close to the surface, hovering then diving, are picking up bait that is being pushed up from beneath by fish. This situation occurs during the "bite" and is the best time to drift fish. When you observe surface activity like this, shut off your motor and drift through or cast into the activity area. Try to remain in the area where the maximum activity is taking place, even if it requires constant moving. Fish your lures close to the surface, often no more than 10 feet down.

Gulls and terns which swoop *gently* down and up again to pick up surface feed are eating plankton or small shrimp. This is probably not an area where you will find great feeding activity by salmon or other fish.

Diving birds such as grebes, cormorants, murres, murrelets and auklets and often indicators of bait fish populations. I believe that these birds can fly close to the surface and detect bait fish concentrations by the odor of rising bubbles. Thus if you see diving birds circling an area and then diving — move in and fish this area. Small divers like murrelets and auklets feed almost exclusively on small bait fish such as minnows and lance. A single murrelet or auklet may indicate that there is feed below. Murres, cormorants and, to a lesser extent, mergansers and western grebes can indicate bait fish populations.

All diving activity by these ducks should be watched closely. Often you will see them with bait fish in their bills as they surface and this will give you a clue as to what type and size of feed is below.

The paths of ducks swimming on the surface will often indicate the movement of feed below. Minnows or herring move offshore in the morning and inshore in the evening. Watch for diving ducks which swim directly above these schools of moving bait fish. It is an excellent idea to take along a good pair of binoculars when driftfishing. These can help you spot surface activity which you might otherwise miss with the naked eye.

Noisy gulls and terns concentrated on the surface while others hover above, periodically folding their wings to dive headlong into the water are working a ball-up or panic-stricken mass of entwined bait fish. Ball-ups do not necessarily indicate that salmon are feeding. There may be dogfish below.

Concentrations of gulls and terns simply swimming about the surface pecking like chickens at grain, are feeding on small crustaceans. Periodically they will take off en masse, circling and settling again to resume the feeding. I have never had any great amount of success driftfishing near surface shrimp populations as driftfishing lures do not represent small shrimp.

BAIT FISH MOVEMENTS

Sand lance generally frequent sand bottoms but will come to the surface in the morning, evening and at tide changes.

Anchovies are like minnows in that they usually frequent surface waters. Unlike minnows or herring however, they come into the shallows by day and swim offshore by night. Herring do the reverse. During evening hours they may come to the surface close to shore where they remain until dawn when they drop in depth as the sunlight increases in intensity. Thus it is at daybreak that fishermen often have the advantage of seeing areas of surface-active bait fish whereas the late-rising fishermen sees nothing because the bait has gone down.

EFFECT OF TIDES

At times, tides have an effect on the bite period. Migratory salmon in Juan de Fuca Strait or the Gulf of Georgia are often geared to activity at certain stages of the tide. Immature feeding salmon that are residents of bays and inlets are often active only in early morning and evening hours, and are not affected too greatly by major tide changes.

In some areas when the tide is falling, all sea life, including seabirds, can be inactive and listless; however, just before the change, activity increases and at the change, or a little after, all "hell" can break loose. In most areas I prefer to fish for one hour before slack water then fish the change and two hours of the flood. However, in many areas, ebb tides are the most productive and it is best to fish after big tides have moved through, in particular fish in the back-eddies after you have had a period of big tides.

With reference to lure weights and tidal flows, I think that you will find that the deeper you fish, the heavier the lure you will have to use. In quiet waters or at slack tide, lure weight is of little importance. People who fish in moving tidal areas usually favor 60 g or heavier size lures. It is important not to fish in one spot too long. If you don't "connect" with fish within 10-15 minutes, move, try another more likely spot, even if it is only 100 or 150 feet away. In late summer or fall months small minnow herring frequent kelp lines and move in schools just outside the kelp.

Use hydrographic charts or depth-sounders to find drop-offs, underwater irregularities, holes, bottom contours, etc. You can

Fishing abrupt drop-offs can be a key to success.

often deduce where salmon and bottom fish are likely to be by just studying a chart.

Whenever possible, take rough landmarks or cross-bearings when you hook a fish. This will permit you to return to the exact spot. If you wish to remain in one spot use your anchor. This works well alongside back-eddies and in rips. If it is difficult or impossible to troll in confined areas (small bays, channels, etc.), you can move in and driftfish with ease.

DEPTH AND TIME OF DAY

Generally speaking, salmon are active during the first two hours of daybreak and last two hours before dark. Migrating fish, especially coho, feed all day, but feed heavily at times associated with tide changes, and often good "bites" occur two or three days after the highest or lowest tides.

In fall, winter and spring months, feeder chinook are found to be fairly active only at daybreak or dusk. Salmon that feed on bait fish during the day will often be in shallow areas in the morning and will seek deeper waters as the day progresses. These salmon will come up towards the surface again in the evening. I have found that the productive driftfishing areas in deep water are the top 10 to 50 feet and the bottom 10 feet. The in-between areas may yield fish, but on average are not consistently productive.

Coho usually frequent depths up to 35 feet, but can feed much

Back eddies are favorite holding areas for salmon.

deeper. I have taken them on deep-trolling sports gear at depths of 200 feet and more. Chinook usually feed and frequent waters down to 90 feet, but can be active feeders even deeper and often near the bottom. Often after salmon have been feeding in upper waters (surface to 35 feet), they will go deep and lie in bottom areas, relaxing so to speak, in areas of minimal tidal flow.

To prolong the "bite," try going down to the bottom with your lure and jigging in some of these areas below where the feeding has occurred; you will often pick up salmon close to the bottom.

WHARF AND BEACH ANGLING

Driftfishing techniques can also be highly successful from the shore or a wharf, particularly in waters which contain large numbers of bait fish. Cast your lure then lift the rod up two to four feet and retrieve line while dropping back the tip. Repeat. This technique gives a lure *wobble-retrieve* and *wobble-sink* action on slack line. Vary length of rod lifts and the speed of line retrieve. Remember not to let the lure sink too deep as you come to the beach (or into shallow water) as it may snag.

NIGHT FISHING

You can catch salmon at night in areas that are floodlit. Lights attract small bait fish and salmon will feed on these at night. Areas to try a "night attack" are off docks, industrial plants, floats, piers and logbooms which are floodlit. In these circumstances you would generally fish by casting or spinning and retrieving your gear fairly close to the surface.

FISHING FROM A SAILBOAT

A driftfish lure of between two and three ounces works well trolled behind a sailboat with speeds ranging from nil to four knots. When becalmed, jig your lure in the conventional manner. A small

sinker may be added to the line in order to obtain some depth when the boat is moving. As with trolling, additional sinkers, if neces-

sary, should be of the slip type (these facilitate landing the fish).
Sinkers should be at least 15 feet upline from your lure.

BOTTOMFISH

I have emphasized salmon not because I feel bottomfish are
second class, either in catching or eating, but because of lim-
itations in space. There is no question that in deeper water areas
and over rocky bottoms you will catch bottomfish at most times.
Driftfish for bottom fish on rock bottoms particularly on incoming
tides. Rockfish, cod, smaller flat fish and even halibut will all
readily take driftfish lures.

I sincerely hope that this section of the book will help fishermen
learn some of the fundamentals of light tackle driftfishing. I hope it
will guide you to success and rewards from angling. You will only
derive from driftfishing what you put into it. Work at it and you will
have success.

PART TWO

Secrets Of Lure Experts

INTRODUCTION

The Buzz-Bomb, Zzinger, Stingsilda, Deadly Dick, Rip Tide, Striker and Laser have become synonymous with the angling style known as driftfishing. In the following section these popular and proven lures are examined by leading experts in the field of driftfishing, often by the very men who invented them.

Doug Field, head of the Buzz-Bomb Lure Corporation, opens the section with a discussion of the famous Buzz-Bomb lure, its invention and the official word on its proper use. As well, he provides an insider's look at the Zzinger needlefish/sand lance and anchovy herring imitations. A better source would be hard to find as Doug invented both versions of the Zzinger.

Sportfisherman **Bob Straith**, owner of a wholesale tackle company, examines the Stingsilda, a Norwegian invention with an interesting West Coast history. As well as providing general information on his favorite driftfishing tactics, Bob also passes along tips on how to modify the Stingsilda to suit your needs.

"**Tats**" **Gatley** hails from Saltspring Island and is the man behind the Deadly Dick, the first true heavyweight spin-fishing lure. "Tats" provides such inside information as which color of Deadly Dick to use at which depth and how to use this well-known lure in various situations, from spin-fishing to stripping and mooching.

Capping off the list of experts, well-known fishing author **Dave Stewart** takes us on a fishing trip with the Reid family, inventors of the Rip Tide, Striker and Laser lures. Speaking directly to the inventors and based on his own experience, Dave provides the low-down on the proper use of these lures.

DOUG FIELD

Doug Field is head of the Buzz-Bomb Lure Corporation, manufac-turer of the popular Buzz-Bomb lures. Since Rex Field invented the first Buzz-Bomb a number of years ago Doug has taken over responsibility for their development, manufacture and marketing around the world. The author also does as much fishing as possible between time spent inventing other successful fishing lures. (See section on the Zzinger lure.)

CHAPTER 7

THE BUZZ-BOMB

By Doug Field

It was a good day. Conditions were just right, with the light ideal and the water perfectly clear. Dozens of chinook were feeding on thousands of herring below the Comox wharf where Rex Field, inventor of the now famous Buzz-Bomb, stood mooching with live herring as he watched the underwater scene unfolding below. The Buzz-Bomb had yet to be born, much less even thought about.

On that day, however, while Rex fished, every so often a lone herring would, as he would say, "buzz-off". Almost immediately a chinook would charge in to gulp down that gyrating, rotating cripple, having singled it out from among the other herring. The exasperating thing for Rex was that the chinook ignored his mooching rig with its docile-looking herring. Time and again he watched re-runs of the show below: a crippled herring, rotating and descending; a charging salmon, ascending with mouth open.

Finally, thinking that a livelier bait would do the trick for him, Rex retrieved his mooching bait and threw it into the sea. Now that half-dead herring rotated as it descended and by the time it had spun down about eight feet, sure enough, a healthy-sized chinook stormed into it.

61

Rex thought this over. Since the herring on his mooching rig had two hooks in it, one fore and the other aft, there was no way for the captive to act like its crippled colleagues. It was always *tied-up*, or *tied-down* so to speak. Although first and foremost a fisherman, Rex had manufactured fishing tackle for more than 20 years. So right there on the wharf, he decided to make a lure which would duplicate the action of his crippled bait that had buzzed-off.

THE FIRST BUZZ-BOMB

He started that same night. And after scrounging up some scraps of lead, stainless steel trolling wire and some swivels, he had

enough materials. All he needed was some sort of mold, so he carved two blocks of wood into the shape he wanted and poured in the molten lead.

The next day, armed with this first Buzz-Bomb, Rex went back to the wharf. He tied his new lure on the line and dropped it slightly below the water's surface, checking its action on a free fall under slack line. It didn't spin properly on the descent, rather it seemed to dart about. The action he had produced was like a glider; the action he wanted was more like a whirly-bird.

Maybe the lure would perform better if the tail flukes were removed. So, out with the knife and off with the flukes. This step stabilized the lure so that it lay substantially horizontal, spinning on its axis as it fell vertically from a slack line. It wasn't perfected yet, but on that first day out it did land three fine winter chinook.

THE PERFECTED BOMB

Rex thought a little more about the spinning action of the crippled herring, the action he wanted for his new lure. This reminded him of a day during his youth. Playing on top of a building under construction, he was throwing unwanted plaster lath boards from the roof to the ground. Each lath, each imaginary bomb, made an audible buzzing or whirring noise as it spun through the air.

The inventor noted the similarity between the spinning bombs of his youth and the rotating herring below the Comox wharf. Could those herring, and his new lure, both give off an audible buzz which attracted salmon? Rex decided to experiment.

The civic marina provided the handiest and perhaps best testing grounds. Because of continuous lighting it was always full of trout, salmon and perch fry feeding day and night. At the marina Rex made an underwater wall by weighting the bottom of a black plastic

sheet and suspending it from a floating 2x4. He then dropped his new lure into the water beside the wall, lifting his rod tip and dropping it to give the bait slack line so it could rotate downward. Almost immediately, dozens of nosy little fish crowded around. And almost as many crowded around on the blind side of the barrier. The lure proved to be a winner.

Until then, anglers had relied upon visual lures, either docile or swimming. But there in the water was a bait that was not only visually stimulating — though in a far different manner because it simulated weakened, crippled easy prey — but a bait giving off some sort of audible vibrations that lured fish from beyond the range of sight. Did it make a sound like his boyhood lath bombs? Maybe. And so it was that Rex combined the notion of noise with the idea of casting bombs when he named his new lure the Buzz-Bomb.

IMPROVEMENTS

The manufacturer and hundreds of interested Buzz-Bombers have spent thousands of hours researching and experimenting to perfect techniques for using this lure and to find the most effective

design and colors. One of the biggest steps was the development of a special alloy by Rex. It makes a ringing noise when tapped. That development alone increased the sound attraction range by about seventy-fold. The writer has also developed models which are designed to "stay down" better in conditions of wind or heavy currents. These include the five-inch, six-inch and eight-inch models which weigh from 3¾ to 16 ounces. Another major development was the perfection of exacting standards for balance and hydro-dynamics.

HOW TO BUZZ-BOMB

Originally the instruction sheet showed four methods of fishing. For clarification the four methods have been narrowed down to the two that are most effective. And though this makes reading quicker, it doesn't always encourage fishermen to pause long enough with their new purchase to really understand the instructions.

When Buzz-Bombing, consider these three points:
• Fish where you think the fish are, where they are known to be, or directly below a mass of bait. With time and practice, you will discover all the places where fish are likely to hang out.

• Lift your rod tip only enough so that when you drop it towards the lure you give it *instant, slack line.* With instant slack, the Buzz-Bomb sinks while rotating horizontally around the axis of your line. Your lift should only be enough so that the Buzz-Bomb falls free for 16 to 18 inches. Once in a while a greater drop serves to call the fish from farther out. This *long distance* call is like the difference between talking and shouting. Raise your rod tip high enough to allow a free fall of about six feet, consequently increasing the sound attraction of the lure.

• Don't jerk the rod tip up too fast. Just raise the rod nice and easy.

When you lift the rod quickly, the line stretches, the rod bends a lot and, when the rod stops, the Bomb shoots up about 10 feet more than necessary. In effect, when you lift the rod tip up fast, it's like shooting the lure out of a slingshot. No fish would take bait moving like that.

HOW TO CATCH MORE FISH

Anyone can use Buzz-Bombs, but it's often the women, children and novices who catch more fish with them. One of the main reasons is that they don't feel they know everything like most of us so-called experts. Moreover, they will read the instructions to get clues about what to do. Then they will do things *right*, like threading the line through the Buzz-Bomb, making sure that the hook or

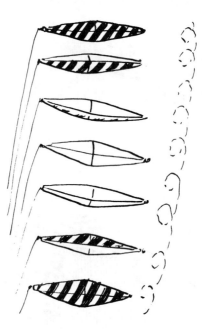

tail end of the Bomb is nearest the loose end of the line. Next, they will thread the line through the small rubber impact bumper, then tie on the hook in the way prescribed on the Buzz-Bomb instruction sheet.

Any pro, of course, would have thrown out the instructions and proceeded to thread his wire leader the wrong way. Maybe he would add a few weights or spinners, or try to bait the hook, when it says right in the instructions not to do those things. Some non-reader may think he'll develop some magic upward darting motion by jerking up like hell and lowering the lure on tight line when, if he'd read the instructions, he'd know this was exactly opposite to the right way. For lack of a better word — alas!

Meanwhile, the women and kids are half asleep, soaking up sun while lazily throbbing the poles up and down. Bango! A fish hits. Their first reaction, in surprise at being caught off guard, is to jump up and jerk the rod. This is all the better because it sets the hook.

Every Buzz-bomber finds himself lifting the rod both faster and higher when he gets excited. The more fish you're catching, the faster you become. It's like getting excited at a hockey game. You yell, scream, jump up and down and wave your arms a lot. Getting excited is what Buzz-Bombing is all about. It shows you're getting the most fun out of fishing. This is especially true when using Method One of the instructions on surface-feeding fish. I've seen some Buzz-Bombers become so enthused while among surface-feeding coho and chinook that they can't even cast straight. I get that way myself sometimes, but it sure beats trolling!

HOW TO BUZZ BOMB

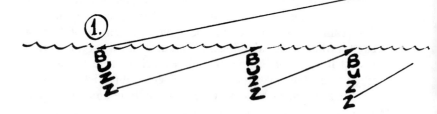

1. FOR LATE SEASON FISHING, CAST
   BUZZ BOMB IN MIDST OF "JUMPERS"
   AND "ROLLERS". RETREIVE/BUZZ
   NEAR SURFACE.

2. BUZZ BOMB MOOCHING -- ONE
   OR TWO 6-FOOT STROKES (*PULL
   UP- DON'T JERK!*) FOLLOWED BY
   SEVERAL SHORT 6- OR 10-INCH
   STROKES.

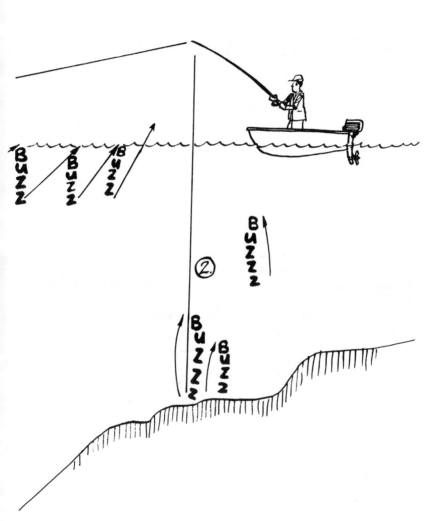

PAY ATTENTION

I've found that the best way to get the most fish and to learn more about fishing per hour on the water is to stand carefully in the boat and just observe, all the time keeping that Bomb coming up and buzzing down.

When fishing Method Two of the instructions you will probably discover that a good many fish strike your Bomb. It may be that you're stopping to talk to fishermen in a nearby boat, or reaching to turn the radio off, but the fact is you have slowed down your action, allowing an observing fish to strike at your lure.

By paying attention to all that's happening around you, you may spot a better location where fish are feeding on top, or birds are diving for bait below. All the time, think of your rod action as simply *lift slow, drop fast, lift slow, drop fast*. Once you've mastered the motion you can forget about it, except when things really become hot and you get excited. That's when you really have to control your timing.

There's no doubt about it; when your motor is off, and you're standing in the boat, both your hearing and vision are increased tremendously. You can hear a flight of gulls far in the distance, or a big fish jumping hundreds of yards away. You can hear the effervescent "fizz" of herring bubbles, when half the time you can't even see them from a moving boat. You may hear a fish splashing behind you, so you turn and see the rings. Perhaps it will jump

again. If, on the other hand, you're sitting in a trolling boat, you'll never see a quarter of what's going on around you. All you'll know is what you observe by sight from your low-flying seat.

When you're standing, Buzz-Bombing, as other boats troll by,

BUZZZ...
PSSST

you will notice fish jumping which the trollers neither see nor hear. It is then that you begin to appreciate why the "buzz" in the Buzz-Bomb is so helpful for catching fish. And if the fish doesn't happen to *see* the bomb, at least it stands a very good chance of hearing and locating it.

CONTROVERSIAL TOPIC

Some people say that the Buzz-Bomb attracts fish into biting it;

others claim that the Bomb aggravates them so much they hit out of anger. It seems evident that both sides are correct. Surely when chinook and coho are no longer feeding, and are no longer enticed by "conventional" trolled tackle, they don't hit the Bomb because they want to dine on it! They hit out of anger; it bugs them. And what of the plankton eaters such as the sockeye and chum salmon? It must bug them, too!

And yet, surface-feeding coho and chinook salmon must surely hit to eat it, because that's exactly what they're there for — food. And fish-eating ducks have no hesitancy in having a smack at the Bomb, so it must be very convincing to them. A number of seals have reportedly taken strikes at the lure and you'd think that they would have a reasonably good brain between those beady black eyes. Herring will bite the Buzz-Bomb too, possibly we theorize, because they feel that it is one of their own, crippled and dying, and sending out "bad vibrations" that will attract larger fish, endangering the rest of the school.

Surprisingly, even sea cucumber and squid will attack Buzz-Bombs. I was amazed to see these most unlikely candidates go after it. I didn't think they had any brains at all.

RECOMMENDED EQUIPMENT

There are basically three categories of equipment recommended for Buzz-Bombing. These will catch any and all types of fish throughout the world, insofar as rod, reel and line are concerned.

In all cases we recommend that the rod be approximately seven feet long and stiffer than the usual rod used for the type of fish sought. Large, oversize guides and tip are best. The bigger the guides and the smaller the diameter of line, the greater the casting range since there will be less friction and the line won't tend to "pile up" behind the guides. The following table will assist in selection of equipment:

TABLE
Represents minimums and maximums

	Small	Medium	Deepwater
Fish size	Up to 3 lbs.	3 to 60 lbs.	Over 35 lbs.
Line size	6-8 lb. mono	15 lbs./20 lbs.	20 lb./60 lb.
Bomb size	2" or 2½"	3"/4"	4"W/5"
Reel size and type	Med. spin-cast	Med. or heavy saltwater spin-cast	Heavy Penn or knuckleduster

When selecting line, compare different brands in the same pound-test size you require. You might be surprised at the amount of variance in the diameters of lines of the same strength, but of different brands. Generally, the poorest quality line is the stoutest. This means the line material is weaker and therefore has to be stouter to achieve the same strength as thinner, better quality line. If you want to be really fussy, borrow a micrometer and gauge several brands before buying. The smaller the diameter, the farther you'll be able to cast your line. Be wary of bargain brands, usually on big spools. They are seldom a bargain.

CHANGE YOUR LINE

Because I fish regularly during hot weather, I usually change my line once a month. The combination of heat, salt, sunlight, incessant casting and retrieving, plus the action of hooked fish twisting on the line all seem to weaken it more quickly in summer than during winter months. Always use fresh line at the start of a fishing season or you'll be telling sad stories about the ones that got away. Since sunlight is fishing line's worst enemy, don't leave your line, spools or rods in the sun unnecessarily.

Because the Buzz-Bomb spins around the line, causing wear, you should re-tie it about once every two hours. You could wait longer, probably, but it's better to be safe. Also, always re-tie before starting to fish.

Every time you catch a fish over five pounds, re-tie the lure. This is important, especially when a fish with sharp teeth, abrasive skin or lots of fight has just been landed.

The best way to re-tie is to slide the Bomb and the bumper up the line about two or three feet. Then, cut the line about six inches below the repositioned lure. Next cut the hook off the piece of line and re-tie it below the lure. For good results, you can use the knot shown here or use other knots that work equally well or better. Try them all.

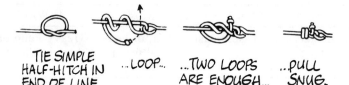

TIE SIMPLE
HALF-HITCH IN
END OF LINE
OR LEADER...

...LOOP...

...TWO LOOPS
ARE ENOUGH...

...PULL
SNUG.

A good trick when tying knots in monofilament line is to wet the last three or four inches with spit or water before starting the knot. The moisture acts as a coolant and lubricant. Without this precaution, the twisting, crimping and friction of pulling the knot tight generates enough heat to cut line strength in half at the knot.

That about sums up the **why** and **how** of Buzz-Bombing. It's my hope that by sharing the story of Rex's invention, you may better understand why it works and how it is supposed to perform for successful fishing. All that's left now is for you to pick up a few Bombs, if you don't already own some, check your gear and take this book along for a handy reference on your next time out.

CHAPTER 8

THE ZZINGER

By Doug Field

Realizing the need for a reasonably priced lure which incorporated both sonic and visual attributes, I developed the Zzinger.

There are two types of Zzingers, these being the Needlefish/ Sand Lance and the Anchovy/Herring. The former is a relatively sleek and thin lure while the latter is a chubbier, more "gutsy" model. A lateral tunnel through the length of the Zzinger accommodates the line direct from your reel or you can pre-assemble Zzingers on leaders with swivels. Starting in the Zzinger's mouth, simply run the line through the tunnel, then thread on the rubber bumper supplied before tying on the hook.

The Zzinger, particularly the Needlefish model, is designed to work well with a single hook. But if you prefer to use a treble hook, then by all means do so.

UNIQUE ACTION

The action built into the Zzinger is quite unique. When given slack line the lure immediately lies on its side and begins to rotate. A moment later the action changes to a combination spiraling and/or darting motion. I call this the duo action descent.

The way to achieve the best action on the Zzinger is to lift the rod gently about six to 12 inches then immediately drop the rod-tip to create slack line. The lure's action is achieved by this free-fall.

Fish that are caught with the hook right down their throat are

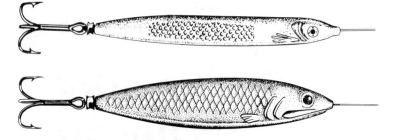

those which bit on the second spiraling/darting action. (The lure is literally crammed down their throats.) Fish hooked in the jaw are generally those which bit the lure in the first, rotating mode.

Excessive darting action can result in hooks catching the main-line above the Zzinger. If this happens, give it less lift and let the lure "bottom out" before commencing the next sequence. Unlike most jigging lures, the Zzinger takes very little lift. Try it beside the boat where you can see what it's doing.

CASTING A ZZINGER

After mooching, the next most popular method is casting. This can be intermixed with mooching so you can cast the lure out and "work" it all the way back until the line is basically beneath the boat or pier.

If there are feeding or rising fish visible, cast your Zzinger just in front and just beyond the head-end of the rising fish. Lift the rod tip smoothly, about two feet. Next, throw the rod tip back towards the lure, creating slack line. Reel in the slack and repeat. If you are fishing a shallow river or wish to stay shallow for other reasons, change your tempo and replace the slow lift with a quick flip. Holding your rod-tip high helps to keep the lure at the surface. In fact, with a half-ounce or 1-ounce Zzinger, you can continually "pop" the surface and fish in as little as 12 inches of water with a little practice. The Needlefish model is the best for casting, and the only model I recommend for river fishing. The Anchovy/Herring model should be reserved for ocean and lake mooching and, if you like, trolling.

For casting and mooching it is best to keep the Zzinger as

straight as possible. It rotates most effectively if straight. Trolling is a different matter, however. Here, a very casual curve in the Zzinger will give it a most productive action. Use slightly less curve to achieve the same action at a higher trolling speed. A bit more curve and you can have the right action for trolling at a dead-slow speed. Experiment!

COLOR SELECTION

Color probably means more to the fisherman than to the fish. Yet, there definitely seem to be certain colors which are preferred by certain types of fish in different areas. My experience indicates that in most places throughout the world, pearlescent white is the most successful color of lure. The addition of various hints of other colors such as blue, pink, black and green seems to improve the effectiveness of some lures, in some waters, for certain types of fish. Practice and experience will dictate which is the best color for your area and the species you seek. I suggest starting with basic white then trying other color combinations from there.

If all the pearly variations are not producing, sometimes the solution is to go to the darker silver/green or silver/blue colors. And if that isn't the solution, then the yellow/green is worth a try. If after all that you are still not happy with the results you are probably in the wrong place. Move and start over again.

On some clear, hot days in midsummer I have found that the silver/green and silver/blue colors outproduce the pearly ones. I believe that this is because the lures are darker and perhaps don't spook the fish as readily as the brighter, whitish pearls.

WHERE TO FISH

Knowing where to fish is one factor which makes some fishermen catch far more fish than others. A depthsounder can be an invaluable instrument for locating the fish. The ideal situation is to find a mass of bait fish and stay with them. Move your boat as the fish move on, and scout around for them when they fade from your sounder. Check the angle of your line as you're fishing. This will indicate which way you're drifting. When the bait disappear from your screen start the boat and head in the direction your line was last pointing. Usually the fish will be there, but not always. If there is a lot of "pushing" by larger fish, it may be hard to stay with the bait for long. But remember, it is at this time, when the pressure is really on, that you'll get your best biting; the big fish are feeding.

It is extremely important to get your lure among the feeding fish

A father and son team proudly display their catch.

right away. Do not doddle. To do this give a little resistance to the line coming off your reel spool and the Zzinger will go down like a rocket. Done properly, a 2½-ounce needlefish Zzinger can reach 240 feet in 30 seconds. When you reach the desired depth, flip the bail and start the lift/drop mode. Be ready anytime, especially on the first lift, to set the hook into a fish.

THE RIGHT DEPTH

Finding the right depth is the key to success with Zzingers, as with most other jigging type lures. If feed is present on the surface, fish just below it. If you have a sounder you'll know where the bottom of the bait mass is, and you'll want to fish a couple of feet below it too. If you find a haystack of bait fish near the bottom, fish just above it. The larger fish often crowd the bait into the bottom before charging through it. This gives the fish the advantage of having the bait "up against the wall," so to speak, where escape is limited to the top and the sides. And of course this is where the feeding fish will be! The big fish also try the same method in reverse, using the surface of the water as an invisible wall.

Another productive place to drop your Zzinger is either above or below a mid-depth band of bait fish as seen on the sounder. On this type of reading, however, most fish are taken just beneath the lower edge of the mass.

If the wind is bucking a fast current, driftfishing is much more difficult. Here again, with a sounder and the right lure at the right depth, you still have a better than average chance of catching fish. And bear in mind that the 2½-ounce (and up) Zzingers are designed to work well in heavy currents and windy conditions. The stronger the wind or current, the heavier the Zzinger you must use.

RIVER FISHING THE ZZINGER

For river fishing try to select the weight of Zzinger which allows you to fish all depths without the loss of too many lures. Cast across the river, usually between five and 20 degrees upstream and work the lure towards you as previously discussed. Likely spots for fish are along the edges of slipstreams, drop-offs leading into pools, and the downstream sides of big rocks. Try to present the Zzinger upstream so that it enters these "fishing holes" at just the right depth. Do not try to cast directly on top of the hot spot.

BOB STRAITH

Bob Straith started fishing at age six and is still fishing 40 years later. He has been actively employed in the tackle industry since 1959, opening his own wholesale tackle company, Brant Industries Ltd., in August 1982.

The Stingsilda lure was invented specifically to deal with the abundant cod supply off the coast of Norway. However, it has also proved highly successful in catching Pacific Coast salmon.

CHAPTER 9

THE STINGSILDA

By Bob Straith

This lure's value to salmon fishermen became apparent through an unexpected incident at Nanaimo on Vancouver Island. Some local Chinese fishermen, in quest of cod, saw the Stingsilda and were delighted with the Norwegian manufacturer's guarantee that the lure "would catch cod, or money refunded." A day later, so the story goes, they marched back to the dealer's shop, angry, and demanding their money back because they had not caught any cod — only masses of salmon. It wasn't long before other locals heard about the Chinese's misfortune and rushed out to buy Stingsildas in the hope that they too would have such "bad luck."

Apparently it was a member of the Norwegian resistance, Asbjorn Horgard, who invented the Stingsilda while in a prisoner-of-war camp. Local cod was the only target he had in mind at that time, now, however, the lure's great catches amongst Pacific salmon have proved an excellent bonus.

JERKING METHOD BEST

Jerking is one of the best methods for fishing with a Stingsilda. The upward movement puts the lure into position, ready to flutter down and get the bite. This is just one method of driftfishing; others are jigging, pulling or mooching.

In addition to its productivity, driftfishing has many other advantages. Constant trolling is neither good for an engine nor efficient, especially with larger models. It is an attractive alternative

for the fisherman to simply shut off his motor and drift along quietly — without shouting to be heard by others in the boat.

MODIFYING LURES

Some fishermen use Stingsildas or any other lure of their choice right out of the package. Others scrape the paint off to expose the lead — remember as a kid when you dropped down a worm and bullheads went straight for the weight first and the worm last — makes you wonder.

Many fishermen apply metallic prism paper to a lure or repaint it. Endless color combinations can be made and if they work for you, stick with them. Color seems to increase success at times.

The fundamental rule for success is to use a lure that is similar to the food being eaten by the fish you want to catch. Size is also an important factor. For example, if the bait fish are four inches, use a four-inch, 40 or 60 gram Stingsilda, but where they are eight inches long use a larger lure of 100 or 125 grams.

Also, the lighter the lure, the lighter the rod. However, if you use too light a rod and a heavy lure, bear in mind that the 'jerk' can be taken up in the rod's bend rather than in actually moving the lure itself.

Some fishermen have increased their catch by reversing the hook on the lure. They switch the splitring and hook to the top or eyed end of the lure, figuring that the bait is swallowed head first by salmon. It's worth experimenting.

GEAR AND TACKLE

It is wise to remember that light, economical gear will, in many

cases, bring in the same number of salmon as can be caught with more expensive equipment.

There is nothing wrong with a four or five-inch troll reel and medium-weight troll rod to start with. You will progress to more sporting outfits as you gain experience and start catching more fish.

Rods: Among the rods I've been comfortable with are Richmake, Eagle Claw, and the latest to enter the market — Silstar Rods of Canada.

As for mooching reels, I prefer the Hardy Longstone or the new Peetz 2000C Moocher.

Hooks: Hooks by Radiant, Eagle Claw or Mustad should be honed sticky-sharp. The E2 Lap Diamond Pen Sharp is just great for hooks and needs no batteries. In electric models I believe that the HyPoint Sharp is best. Eagle Claw trebles (674B Extra) are the best-hooking treble and have the added quality of bending straight when hooked on the bottom. This gives you a good chance of getting your lure back.

Some fishermen argue that if a fish snaps your line, stainless hooks take longer (if ever) to dissolve. This can kill the fish, whereas non-stainless hooks tend to rust out faster.

Hooks 1/0, 1, and 2 (in treble sizes) will catch most weights of fish, as hook sizes do not seem to alter one's success ratio. Also, being silver they tend to help attract fish.

Size 4, 5 and 6 stainless splitrings by Radiant Lures fit most sizes of stingers, are very strong and don't rust.

Line There are many good monofilaments on the market. I prefer

to use the Les Davis Super Velux Line (12 to 20 pounds) or Maxima Super Soft. They are strong, durable and of excellent knot strength.

A good way to keep twists out of your line is to use a small swivel, plain barrel or ball bearing. This way a 20-pound main line can be fished twist-free with a 15-pound test leader to the lure. The leader can be anywhere from six inches to 12 feet; the length does not seem to matter.

FAMILY FUN

Drifting and fishing is tailor-made for family fun as it allows

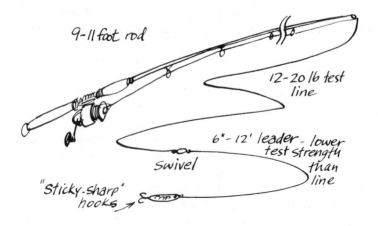

9-11 foot rod

12-20 lb test line

6"-12' leader - lower test strength than line

swivel

"Sticky-sharp" hooks

several lines to be fished simultaneously. To avoid tangles, keep the rods apart. As soon as one person has a strike, the others should quickly haul in their lines and clear the decks for action. Tangles, by the way, are not as frequent in driftfishing as in trolling, but if they do happen both fishermen should simply play the same fish. A fish in the boat is certainly worth a tangle.

If there is a swell running and your arm's getting tired, try putting

your rod into the holder and letting the boat jig for you. You'll have to be prepared to move fast to grab the rod and set the hook since the boat "jerk" is usually not quick and hard enough to set it firmly on its own.

KEY TO SUCCESS

The key to successful driftfishing is to position yourself over some bait fish such as minnows or anchovies. You only have to wait, as sooner or later the salmon will come to feed.

All you do is raise your Stingsilda, then let it flutter down. This downward movement will imitate the motion of a wounded bait fish that can no longer stay with the rest of the school. Such a fish will be attacked by predators such as salmon which strike at wounded or weak members of their target species almost automatically, even if their bellies are full of feed.

Ticks, touches, bumps or hits are often the signs of a fish making a pass at the lure. The salmon will mouth the lure, then discovering that it is a foreign metal object, will reject it. It is in that moment

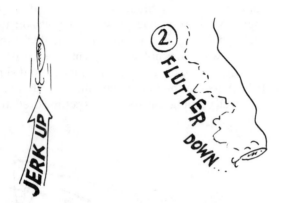

before the lure is rejected that you must jerk your rod and set the hook fast.

VARY YOUR METHODS

Alternating from jigging to trolling can make for an enjoyable day's fishing. This gives the fish a change from perpendicular falling bait to bait being trolled horizontally. In any case, if the bite goes off, be adaptable — the fish sure are.

There is always some lure or method to entice a hit. Try your own ideas. Experiment. Elaborate on what you already know.

If you like stripping, it helps to strip your gear to the surface in jerks since the salmon will sometimes follow your lure up. Then reverse the process and let out your line. Also, when letting the line down to a desired depth, it pays to strip down in jerks as the line is falling. A salmon might be 10 feet under your boat, or 100 feet away.

When you are not sure just how deep the fish are, let each person in the boat fish at a different depth until someone connects. Or if you are by yourself, jig your way to the bottom, then back to the surface, taking a minute or two at each depth. That is, jig at 20 feet, 30, 40, 50 and so on, until you hook a fish. Then return to the depth where you hooked it; where there's one, there's usually another.

If you find you have to jig in depths of 60 to 100 feet, the brown Maxima lines work best as they are tough and stretch-resistant. Also, when a salmon is hooked at depths over 70 feet (salmon have a more lively strike than bottom fish), react fast and hard, raising your rod as high as possible and wind (or strip) line in quickly as the salmon heads toward the surface. You'll want to keep pace with it to ensure the hook remains firmly implanted in its mouth.

Your main problem is to find a concentration of salmon and be at the right depth, with the right gear and a little luck when the bite comes on. Look for the bait birds, terns, murres, garnets, cormorants, and their frenzied feeding patterns. They will give you an indication of where the fish are. However, the decision on where to fish is up to you.

If there are no salmon to be had, try another species: Bottom fish for instance are especially susceptible to jigging. Halibut can also be taken, particularly if the lure is kept very close to a sandy, shallow bottom and jigged a little slower. Sole, of the same family, can also provide a lot of excitement for the wee folk during a hot afternoon on a slow flood tide. (Use a small lure as sole have tiny mouths.)

"TATS" GATLEY

"Tats" Gatley: Saltspring Island resident and fisherman."Tats" Gatley has developed and tested several fishing lures over the years. One of the most popular of these is the Deadly Dick which he developed and fish-tested in the early 1950s. Manufactured in Victoria, B.C., by Victoria Plating, they are still in wide use. "Tats" points out that though the following fishing techniques pertain especially to the Deadly Dick, they can be modified and applied to most other driftfishing lures.

CHAPTER 10

THE DEADLY DICK

By "Tats" Gatley

The Deadly Dick was introduced to the Pacific coast in the early 1950s. It was the first of the true heavyweight spin-fishing lures, as opposed to casting spoons which had been adapted from trolling spoons.

It is an adaptable lure which can be fished in any number of ways. Recommended colors to have on hand include:

- Nickel: for deep water.
- Green: for 50 to 75-foot depths.
- Pink: for 15 to 50-foot depths.
- Yellow: for fish that are feeding deep beneath a herring school.
- Red: for shorelines and around estuaries — particularly good for fall fishing.
- White: with red spots. Good general purpose lure.

There are 12 models available, ranging in weight from one-sixteenth of an ounce to 3 ounces in regular sizes, and long versions up to five inches in length.

When using standard Deadly Dick casting lures (half, three-quarter, one or two ounces) for salmon, the following techniques are recommended:

FISHING FROM A BOAT

When spin-fishing from a boat, anchor near or tie up to a kelp bed. Cast out and allow the lure to sink to a depth at which you

believe fish are feeding. Reel in at a moderate rate then *stop*. Jig once or twice, then give a jerk or jig. Continue as before. Fish will usually take the lure just as you begin to wind in.

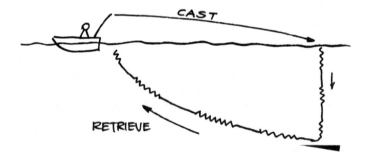

If fishing alongside a tide rip, cast out; allow your lure to swing around to the edge; lower and raise the rod slowly two or three

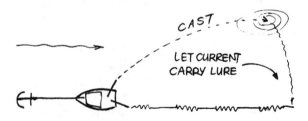

times, then wind in six to ten feet. Repeat until your lure is fully retrieved. If salmon are seen to follow the lure but will not strike, change to a Deadly Dick one size smaller.

If fishing right in the tideway, place your rod in the rod holder and let the lure stream astern 30 to 50 feet. Now sit down and every

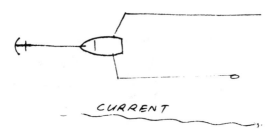

CURRENT

so often gently rock the boat from side to side, retrieving about six feet of line — by hand — without removing the rod from the holder. Let it go again and repeat the procedure.

When fishing from shore, cast out and allow the lure to sink, then reel in fast, stop, jig and repeat. Vary your speed of return constantly.

GRAB!

STRIPPING

For this procedure try using a half- or one-ounce standard Deadly Dick or Number One or Two long. Use a nine-foot rod (with trigger guide), 15 to 20-pound test soft nylon line, and a single-action reel such as the Daiwa 275, Zebco 300 or Hardy

Longstone. Your forefinger should be just in front of the guide.

Cast about 60 to 75 feet. Allow the lure to sink (vary your depth) then strip in by hand, letting the line lie in the bottom of the boat. Vary your retrieves with fast, little tugs and some long pulls — always by hand. Your rod should be held fairly low; a ''sloppy

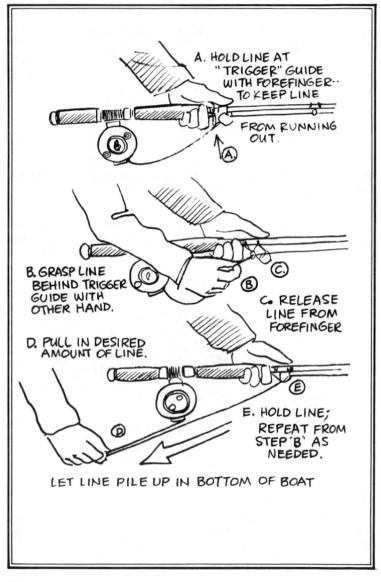

A. HOLD LINE AT "TRIGGER" GUIDE WITH FOREFINGER·· TO KEEP LINE FROM RUNNING OUT.

B. GRASP LINE BEHIND TRIGGER GUIDE WITH OTHER HAND.

C. RELEASE LINE FROM FOREFINGER

D. PULL IN DESIRED AMOUNT OF LINE.

E. HOLD LINE; REPEAT FROM STEP "B" AS NEEDED.

LET LINE PILE UP IN BOTTOM OF BOAT

Joe" method of handling it often pays off if a fish makes its hit under the boat (which it often does). Set the hook hard, then allow the fish to run until all the loose line is out and then play from the reel as usual.

MOOCHING A DEADLY DICK

Place rods in holders at an angle of about 45 degrees to the boat and at a 35 degree elevation. Use the oars, for in this method most of the action of the lure is controlled by your manipulation of the boat.

This is what happens when you pull on the oars...

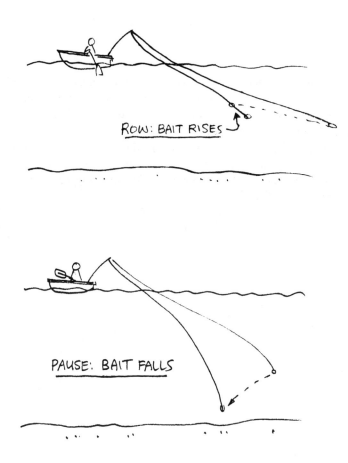

ROW: BAIT RISES

PAUSE: BAIT FALLS

By alternatively rowing and stopping, you can make your lure take the following path...

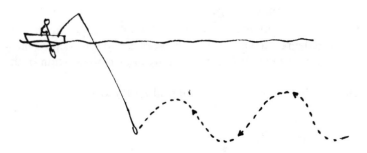

Let us carry this one step further by *not* rowing in a straight line. Your lure will now perform all sorts of crazy antics under the water, a very close approximation of a wounded bait fish.

THE LONG DEADLY DICK

Long Deadly Dick casting lures, in sizes one to four, are primarily used when jigging for salmon. You need a fairly stiff rod, nine to 10 feet long, with a large capacity spinning reel and 15 to 25-pound test line.

Cast and allow your lure to sink. Remember, the Long Deadly Dick is specially designed to fish *going down* and *coming up*. Feed the line but stop the descent occasionally. You now have a pattern like this:

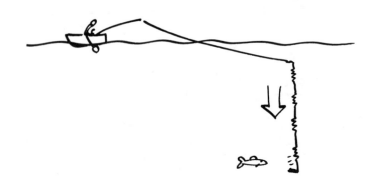

If you start winding when the lure is near the bottom you will achieve the following underwater pattern:

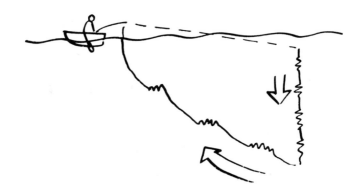

The importance of fishing the lure correctly, either through rod control or reel control, cannot be over-emphasized. With a little practice, a variety of underwater patterns can be developed. This adds another dimension to one's fishing pleasure by removing saltwater angling from a game of chance to one of skill.

Jig-fishing for salmon is also effective from docks, off rocks into rip-tides or any place where it is necessary to get down to the fish.

When mooching with the Long Deadly Dick, a proven technique is for someone else to row while you hold the rod. When using this method, even more lift can be put into the lure by jigging and/or occasionally stripping.

Although the Long Deadly Dick was never designed for trolling, many have tried and successfully adapted it to this form of fishing. The Number One and Two lures are particularly good when fished behind a dodger or flasher in exactly the same way as any other trolling lures. The Number One Deadly Dick should be used 32 inches and the Number Two about 36 inches behind the dodger or flasher.

DAVE STEWART

Dave Stewart was born in Revelstoke and spent the first years of his life in his family home above the cairn marking the driving of the last spike at Craigellachie. His earliest recollection of those years is of holding his Dad's fly rod whilst a small trout danced wildly across a foaming pool in Gorge Creek. That trout was a cutthroat, which perhaps accounts for his admiration for these fine fish.

Moving throughout B.C., first with his parents and later as a CPR telegraph operator, Dave saw a lot of B.C., mostly from villages and small towns where fishing was his main pastime. His wife, Joyce, and five children tagged along.

Infected by the writing virus early in the 1950s, Dave began to look further afield for subject matter, and over the years has gained a greater overall knowledge of this province and its fishing than most anglers. He has fished all the Canadian provinces and territories (with the exception of the Maritimes) and has had some experience in the United States, Africa and Mexico.

Dave and his wife live in Ladysmith on Vancouver Island where they both do a lot of fishing. Dave was Field Editor of BC OUT-DOORS for six years.

CHAPTER 11

THE RIP TIDE, STRIKER AND LASER

By Dave Stewart

In Sansum Narrows, just off world-famous Cowichan Bay, the tide-rips are rambunctious. They are especially noticeable where they swirl around and over underwater reefs. These reefs provide breakwaters against the eddies and fast-moving water where bait fish and squid congregate. Here, chinook salmon (and other predators) come to feed among the hapless, bunched forage, lying just below the fast currents.

Hugh Reid and his son Ken had fished those waters for many years. They knew just where the fish held... and also knew firsthand just how difficult it was to get a bait or lure down to the fish through those swirling tide-rips. So they started making heavy lures, utilizing various designs and materials, aiming for something which would get down past those treacherous currents to the fish. It then, of course, had to be capable of enticing those fish to bite!

TRIAL AND ERROR

After varying degrees of success and failure, the Reids finally settled on the S-shaped, oval-bodied, Rip Tide lures now familiar to thousands of B.C. saltchuckers. Its high ratio of weight-to-surface-area allowed it to penetrate heavy tide-runs, yet still provide action enough to tease fish into striking.

It became obvious to the Reids that a lure as heavy as the Rip Tide would often tear out of the mouths of hard-fighting salmon if the hook was fastened solidly to the lure. So they made a hole

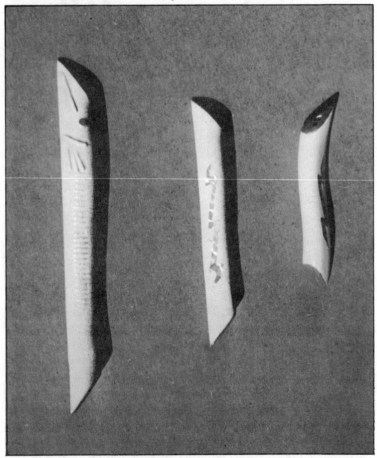

The Striker, Laser and Rip Tide.

through each Rip Tide from end to end. Threaded on a leader, topped with a good, free-turning swivel and tipped with a split-ring-mounted hook with the knot protected from the lure by a plastic "bumper," the Rip Tide ran free along the leader.

BROUGHT IN LIMITS

Although the Reids perfected the Rip Tide lures essentially for their own use, it soon became obvious to local fishermen that they had something good going for them. All too often, when they returned with empty boats, Ken and his father brought in limits. Pestered by friends and others to provide them with these killer lures, Ken started packaging the lures and placing them in local stores.

The Rip Tide was rapidly becoming a best seller. Ken, however, had ideas for variations on the original design. He developed a longer, slimmer version of the Rip Tide which he named "Striker." He also added a few innovations such as prism strips along each side, and a greater variety of colors along the back.

The Striker soon proved to be an even hotter item than the Rip Tide and soon outsold the original. By that time the "Rip Tide salute" (the quick raising and lowering of rods) was becoming familiar in Cowichan waters.

FULL-TIME JOB

And for Ken, what had been an interesting pastime suddenly became full-time work, manufacturing, testing, promoting and selling the new lures. Salmon fishermen from Victoria to Nanaimo were using the new lures with great success and they were even showing up as far away as Campbell River and Port Alberni. Nor had anglers from B.C.'s most heavily populated area overlooked a good bet; stores in and around Vancouver started selling Rip Tides and Strikers.

Ken didn't sit on his laurels, however. He started work on a still longer and slimmer drift-lure. He calls it the "Laser" and it too is proving popular all along the coast.

I became a confirmed Rip Tide and Striker addict a couple of years back, the first time I gave them a serious test. Although I had bought a few Rip Tides "on spec" some time before, I hadn't really learned how to use them. When Ken invited me to go fishing with him, I agreed, but insisted on fishing with my collection of various other types of drift-lures, against Ken and his lures. After two hours without catching a single fish, while Ken and Chemainus angler Roy Knight filled a tub, I switched. I caught fish immediately, and that was convincing. I had become a Striker fan for sure.

VALUABLE TIPS

Although I consider myself reasonably proficient with Rip Tide lures, I got in touch with Ken before writing this chapter and asked him to make a few recommendations for prospective Rip Tide, Striker and Laser users. Here is a brief outline of Ken Reid's techniques:

• Birds, particularly gulls, are a good sign of feeding fish. Don't go charging in among them, however. Try to locate the edge of the bait fish and fish there. Try just above the bait first, then drop down to just below it.

• Leaders should suit the rod. A long mooching rod, for instance, can handle a leader six feet or so long, whereas a short spinning rod needs a much shorter leader. Use the size of treble hook supplied with the lure as it will perform best. A good ball-bearing or bead-chain swivel is absolutely necessary to prevent line-twist. Renew the leader every time you go out, and re-tie the hook every time you boat a large fish. Be sure that all three hooks are needle-sharp before starting ... and keep them that way. If you lose more than one fish in succession, put on a new, sharp hook.

• For chinook or cod, simply drop the lure overside to the desired depth. If you aren't sure where the fish are, start around 12 fathoms (70-75 feet). For winter springs, drop a Rip Tide lure right to the bottom, then pull it up two fathoms (12 feet). Drop the rod-tip to the water, then bring it up smartly. Hesitate a second or so at top of swing, then drop it just as fast. Keep repeating, but watch line carefully on the drop. Ninety per cent of strikes happen as the lure flutters downward. If you feel even a slight bump or pull, jerk hard. Even after you have a fish on, give another hard pull to make sure the hook is set. Chinooks, especially large ones, have hard mouths.

• For coho, start fishing between five and seven fathoms (30-40 feet), using lighter lures than those needed for chinook. Forty to 60 g work well for most coho and can easily be cast to where fish are feeding on or near the surface. Incidentally, as a rule of thumb, figure one foot of depth for one gram of weight when using Rip Tide, Striker or Laser lures. Thus, for 30 to 50 feet, use 40 g — for 60 or 70 feet, use 60 g — and so on.

• Fish for cod on reefs or close to rockpiles. Locate bottom, pull

100

Don't be surprised if salmon aren't the only fish you catch driftfishing, many species will take a driftfish lure.

lure up two or three feet, then work it with much shorter pulls than for salmon. Two feet is a good pull to start with.

• A too-heavy lure will outfish one that is too light. This is very noticeable where currents belly the line out. This not only interferes with the fast-dropping, "flutter action" but makes setting the hook much more haphazard.

• Rip Tide, Striker and Laser lures come in ten weights from 28 to 145 g. Seven colors include yellow, green, blue, red, pink, black and all-white. If you know there are fish around but nothing is hitting, try another color. Above all, keep in mind that all rules are made to be broken. If one doesn't work for you, try your own idea. That's what makes driftfishing interesting.

PART THREE

Expert Advice On Fish and Fishing

INTRODUCTION

All the technical fishing know-how in the world won't help the angler catch fish if he doesn't know something of their habits and the clues needed to locate them. In this final section, three of the best-known and top fishermen on the coast share their secrets on salmon habits, how to locate feeding salmon and how to catch them.

Filmmaker, author and fishing expert **Charlie White** starts the section with a detailed look at the clues which tip top fishermen to the location of bait fish and feeding salmon. Using information gleaned from his famous underwater film footage of striking salmon, Charlie passes on the tricks and tips to successful salmon fishing.

Outdoor writer and fishing pro **Lee Straight** takes a close look at the means and methods of successful mooching for Pacific salmon. His chapter is a step-by-step guide to the hows and whys of mooching, covering everything from rods, leaders, sinkers and hooks to boats and when and how to set the hook.

Charter fishing guide, ex-broadcaster and light-tackle expert **Ted Peck** closes the book with solid information on the life and habits of chinook and coho salmon as well as a professional's advice on how to catch them. Ted covers such basics as identification and feeding patterns — invaluable information for the sportsman — as well as the keys to successful fall and winter fishing and a selection of his own valuable tips on light-tackle fishing for salmon.

CHARLIE WHITE

Charlie White is an internationally known author, filmmaker and fish behavior researcher. He has written seven books on the subject of salmon and other marine life, with sales totalling 400,000 copies.

He has worked as a biologist/photographer with the Oregon Fish Commission, and spent three summers as a charter fishing guide on Vancouver Island where he gained a reputation for consistent success using light tackle.

He conceived and developed the Undersea Gardens, a unique aquarium in reverse where the public can descend beneath the sea to watch marine life in its natural habitat. (Four Undersea Gardens were eventually built in Canada and the United States.)

For the past 10 years Charlie has been researching salmon strike behavior with a unique remotely-controlled underwater camera. His research is shedding new light on how fish react to various lures and his work is debunking many popular theories on salmon behavior.

He has produced two feature length films on salmon behavior. One, "Salmon Spectacular!" has played to sellout crowds across North America and his most recent film "In Search of the Ultimate Lure" was scheduled to be distributed world-wide starting in the fall of 1985.

Charlie lives on the waterfront near Sidney, B.C. where he catches salmon, crabs and other marine life within sight of his front door.

CHAPTER 12

FISHING LORE

By Charlie White

Without a background of fishing lore, many of the nitty-gritty details don't make much sense. Dealing with a quarry that lives in a world almost completely alien to us, our fishing techniques have necessarily been developed primarily by trial and error. Even then, our conclusions have been based almost entirely on circumstantial evidence. Until I began my work with a remote-controlled underwater television camera, we had not been able to see the salmon actually take our lure, except for rare occasions near the surface, which is often just a blur, swirl or splash.

Our underwater camera has shown us that more salmon are looking at our lure than we ever dreamed. More than 90 per cent of the fish that approach turn away without striking. Of those that strike, more than half throw the hook before we realize they have had the lure in their mouths. (Sharpening hooks until they are "sticky sharp" can cut the number of lost fish in half according to our camera research. So, sharpen those hooks!)

Our underwater research is helping us discover a great deal more about fish behavior and which lures salmon like best. (Details of these findings can be found in a forthcoming book entitled "In

Search of the Ultimate Lure.'' They will also be presented in a film of the same name.)

Moreover, fisheries departments in B.C., Oregon, Washington and the Great Lakes region are gathering a growing amount of data on habits and needs of the salmon. Hopefully these studies will give us new information on the migrating and feeding habits of salmon to help us solve the first, most time-consuming aspect of fishing. This is, of course...

FINDING SALMON

Native Indians, commercial fishermen, charter boat guides and keen sportsmen have all contributed to the considerable fund of knowledge needed to find salmon.

Looking for surface activity and interpreting its meaning is one prime way to zero in on feeding schools of fish. Bait fish milling on the surface is an encouraging sign, but herring and candlefish boiling frantically right out of the water is a *sure* sign of something feeding on them from below.

Diving birds (murres, murrelets, auklets, etc.) might be pushing up the feed, but you can quickly determine if this is the case since they seldom stay underwater for more than a minute. If there are

...YOU WOULDN'T CONSIDER STAYING IN THIS NICE, FRESH WATER -- WHERE WE CAN KEEP AN EYE ON YOU...?

no diving birds, then the bait is being attacked by salmon, dogfish or even rockfish or ling cod. Salmon or dogfish are the most likely prospects, and you may have to troll through the bait to determine which one it is unless you see the telltale fin of the shark-like dogfish.

Even if you see dogfish, it does not mean that salmon are not present. We often see both salmon and dogfish (as well as bottom fish and diving birds) attacking ball-ups of herring and anchovies at the same time.

WATCH HERRING

Herring or candlefish ball-ups where bait fish instinctively gather together in a tight, round ball of living flesh are another sure sign of feeding predators. The herring all try to get to the center of the ball while the birds or fish slash away at the luckless ones on the outside. The predators may also push right through the ball-up. I can remember watching a huge sphere of small herring with no attackers in sight, then suddenly the head of a large dogfish appeared from *inside* the herring ball. He swam lazily out into the clear, his jaws dripping with half-eaten carcasses.

Schools of surface feed and ball-ups are usually, but not always, spotted first by the hungry eyes of nearby seagulls. They cruise most fishing areas like a fleet of patrol planes, watching for signs of food from their high vantage point. When they spot something, they dive to investigate, then squawk the news loudly if they find bait fish. I've always wondered why they make this raucous shout, since it attracts the rest of the flock which sometimes muscle in and

steal the catch of the original scout. It must be an instinct designed for the survival of the group as a whole.

TELL-TALE GULLS

Watching seagulls will keep you informed of any meaningful surface activity. This is especially important when fishing for the

shallower-feeding coho. After spotting some feeding gulls, you must then determine what they are eating. Rex Field, former resident fishing genius at Comox, B.C. gave me some fascinating information on what can be learned from watching feeding gulls.

For instance, according to Rex, when you see a large gull being chased by another, you can be pretty sure that the herring are large, probably six to seven inches. How can you draw that conclusion? Well, the big herring can't be swallowed easily, even by the large gulls, so they often get stuck halfway down. One gull chases another to steal the herring out of its mouth.

111

Small herring or candlefish are easily swallowed, so there is seldom any chasing by the larger birds. The small gulls are almost always feeding on these smaller bait fish, said Rex, since they have too much trouble handling larger sized food. If small birds are just sitting on the water, pecking at something just below the surface, this indicates the presence of concentrations of tiny shrimp or shrimp-like organisms.

Knowledge about the *size* of bait fish is vital information if we are to be successful anglers. If we can't actually see the bait jumping, or in the mouth of a gull or diver, Rex Field's tips can help determine bait size. Matching this size with your lure is important. Feeding salmon seem to prefer lures of the same general size as the feed they are working at the time. Their instinctive striking urge is more easily triggered by a lure which looks like one of the herring it may have wounded.

DEPTH GAUGE

Birds can give you a clue about how deep to fish. For instance, if gulls are the only birds present, the feed is just below the surface. If small diving birds (murrelets, most likely) are with the gulls, the bait fish will probably be 15 to 25 feet underwater. The murrelets will periodically force the feed up to the surface where the gulls can get at them. Murrelets won't, however, push deep-running herring

GULLS ONLY

GULLS AND DIVING BIRDS

DIVING BIRDS ONLY

15 to 25 Feet

To 100 Feet

all the way to the surface and if this is the case gulls won't hang around.

It follows then that diving birds alone mean that the bait is quite deep, often 100 feet or more. "I've caught diving birds at 100 feet on a Buzz-Bomb," said Rex.

Other experts use the presence of birds in slightly different ways to determine fishing depth. Jim Gilbert, third generation professional guide of the famous fishing family, says that he has even timed the divers underwater. By counting how long the birds remained under, he has developed estimates on relative depths of feed and salmon.

FISH INTELLIGENCE

Frustrated anglers give fish credit for figuring out all sorts of things to outwit luckless fishermen. Nonsense! Salmon live entirely by instinct. Their whole life cycle is determined by a series of

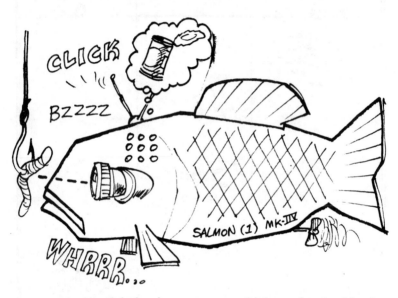

pre-programmed behavior patterns which evolved with the species.

They strike at a lure because a "trigger" in their tiny brain is activated by a certain sight, sound or smell. They don't look at a lure and say to themselves, "Is that really a herring or is it a fake?" If your lure doesn't trigger the strike reaction, it might just as well be a piece of driftwood.

So matching bait size helps get more strikes. A salmon feeding on small herring may not "trigger" at all when a big seven-inch bait comes rolling by. At other times, however, it may grab the bigger lure. This is one reason why it is helpful to examine stomach contents of the fish you catch. It will tell you the bait the salmon are naturally feeding upon at that time.

Sometimes size is not very important, but on other occasions it can be critical. If the salmon are working on a school of candlefish (needlefish, sand lance), it is often vital to match the shape as well as the size of the feed. The long, narrow spoons, bucktail flies or flashtails will take fish, especially coho, in this situation, while a wider spoon of the same size or color will be completely ignored.

SHRIMP

The tell-tale, little V-shaped ripples moving in the water beside your boat indicate the presence of tiny shrimp. What can you do when salmon are feeding on these tiny critters? You can't match their ant-like size with any natural or artificial lure but you can try to imitate their color and perhaps the general *action*. Bucktail flies, flashtails, hootchies and other "hairy" or flutter-tail lures are usually most productive at these times. Pink, ginger, red or shades of grey approximate the color of most shrimp-type feed.

FOOD CHAIN

These tiny organisms are usually the second step in the great food chain of the sea. This food chain is the basis of all life in the

115

oceans and some understanding of it will help us catch more fish. The chain starts with the microscopic plankton which are nourished by the minerals and other chemicals in the sea. Plankton can be either plant or animal, *algae* being the basic plant plankton. The term plankton is also applied to many tiny animal forms, including the larvae of many larger marine creatures. Crab larvae, for instance, are often abundant in June, frequently becoming a temporary foodstuff for coho and consequently causing a slump in coho catches.

Since plankton is the base of the whole food chain, its abundance determines the numbers of larger creatures which can survive in an area. The Pacific Northwest corner of the United States and along the B.C. coast through Alaska is one of the richest ocean areas in the world. The relatively heavy rainfall and large river systems pour a continuous supply of rich minerals and nutrients into the sea. This nourishment, combined with sunlight and favorable water temperatures and currents, provide ideal plankton habitat.

Plankton have little, if any, power of locomotion and are at the mercy of the tide and currents to carry them around. Tidal back-eddies create natural gathering places for plankton. It is swept into those areas out of the main current where it circles around in the back-eddy or just settles. These concentrations of plankton attract

larger organisms, which in turn attract the herring and other bait fish. The foraging salmon usually locate the bait in short order.

For this reason salmon fishing is often best in areas where such back-eddies form — off points of land, behind islands, near reefs and sharp drop-offs, or near narrow passes between islands. When you can't see surface activity to guide you to the fish, such spots should be your first choice. This is especially true with chinook since these larger salmon do not feed on the surface as often as coho.

VERTICAL EDDIES

Sometimes the eddy is vertical, rather than horizontal. The water pours over a shallow reef, sand bar or shelf and rolls down

and around behind it. This creates the same plankton and bait gathering conditions as with a horizontal eddy, though the edges of

the eddy are not as clearly defined. Often the best indication is a boiling or "welling-up" on the surface.

Back-eddies can be so large it is hard to recognize them, except from a low-flying plane. For instance, the whole area east and north of Tumbo Island is a hugh eddy when the tide floods around

Saturna Island into the Strait of Georgia. A similar big backwater forms off the south end of Whidbey Island in Puget Sound.

PLANKTON MOVEMENTS

Rex Field had some interesting thoughts on why the salmon sometimes move out into the center of Georgia Strait. He noted that the big tides (large rise and drop) cause fast currents which push the plankton and feed close to shore in quieter waters behind such places as Hornby Island. On the smaller tides, the plankton drift more freely out into the center of the strait and salmon follow suit.

The size of a tide change is also helpful in determining fishing depth. Fish are lazy. They won't work if they don't have to. So if they aren't hiding in a slow-moving back-eddy during a fast-running tide, they'll tend to move closer to the bottom where current speed is less.

This is one of the reasons why salmon tend to feed better as slack tide approaches. As water movement slows, the bait fish and the salmon find it easier to swim around in search of food. They also tend to move up nearer the surface. With salmon at various depths and on the move, your chances of catching fish are obviously improved.

Speaking of depth, coho are often found in the top 30 feet of water. However, my recent downrigger fishing tests have come up

with coho at surprising depths. We hooked a beauty early one July morning at 85 feet in an area where we thought the coho were almost always shallow. We have had a similar experience at Active Pass where we used to get them right on top. Incidentally, a coho hooked deep on a downrigger usually explodes from the water in a

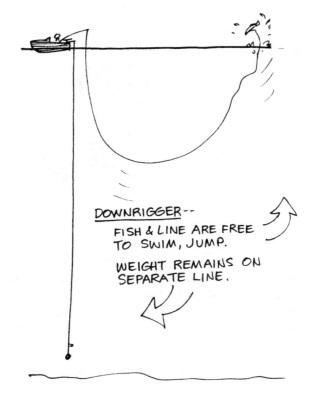

DOWNRIGGER--
FISH & LINE ARE FREE
TO SWIM, JUMP.

WEIGHT REMAINS ON
SEPARATE LINE.

spectacular jump after a rush from the bottom. That's one of the beauties of downriggers; after the fish trips the release, there is nothing to hold it down!

DEEP-RUNNING COHO

Perhaps a new race of deep-running coho is evolving. The shallow-running fish are the ones most likely to be caught by the nets and lures which drop down from the surface. Therefore, if the deep-running salmon are the ones that get to the spawning grounds generation after generation, their progeny are also likely to be deep

fish. Nature's law of survival of the fittest indicates that, in this case, man-made pressures are modifying the coho's habits.

The same thing seems to be happening to the already deep-running chinook. They are being caught deeper than ever, especially by commercial fishermen who are catching large ones at 500 feet or more. Sportsmen are also going to unusual depths with mooching gear, wire lines or downriggers to get the chinook. Some reports indicate that sport-caught chinook are being taken at 250 feet.

WHY FISH STRIKE

There are many theories on how to trigger that instinct to strike, but the most sensible, in my opinion, is the *predator* analogy. Through all of nature's realm the predators have one basic function: to weed out the weak, sick or inefficient members of their target species.

Wolves and cougars stalk the elk and deer herds watching for the weak or young which get separated from the main group. If they attack the healthy ones in desperation, they often have an unhappy time. An old-time trapper told me the story of how he watched a hungry wolf pack attack a healthy bull elk. The elk shook the wolves off his back, kicked and gored them until they slunk away in defeat to lick their wounds.

A government biologist tells the story of watching a flock of ducks in which one duck was faltering and falling out of formation. A large hawk suddenly appeared and headed straight for the straying duck, bumping into a healthy bird on the way. But the hawk ignored the healthy duck and went on to catch the weakened one, illustrating once again that predators go for the injured members of any group.

Salmon will prey on anything they can catch, but herring, anchovies, candlefish, shrimp and squid make up the majority of their diet. Salmon attack a huge school of feed by charging straight into it, their mouths agape, trying to catch as many as possible.

This head-long rush, propelled by powerful sweeps of the tail, also stuns and injures herring which get in the way. These injured herring are then prime targets for other hungry salmon.

When we troll, cast or mooch our lure among a school of thousands of bait fish, we don't have much chance of attracting the salmon unless our bait stands out from the crowd. We do this by giving our lure the erratic action of a wounded herring. The salmon

sees our bait; its predatory instincts flash a signal, and *wham!* — it grabs the lure in the midst of thousands of healthy herring.

UP-TO-DATE DATA

Owing to the extreme unpredictability of salmon fishing, the most valuable information one can have is recent data, hot from the landing net. This tells you what the salmon are doing right now.

One of the few advantages of the ever-increasing number of boats is the reference information they can provide. When another boat catches a fish, you should find out as much as possible to guide your own efforts.

When I see a salmon landed, I try to maneuver near the successful boat. After congratulating the angler, I quickly ask the pertinent questions:

• *"What did you catch it on?"* I follow-up with questions on lure color, size, etc. if the first answer is too general.

• *"How much weight were you using?"* This gives you only a general indication since many factors effect lure depth. However, any information about weight when combined with details on line length will be of real help in zeroing in on the fish. (Wire line equipment also effects depths, but you can often tell this from observing the rod and reel used.)

124

• *"How much line out?"* He will reply in terms of feet or "pulls" (about 18 inches).

Such sharing of information makes good sense. Freshwater

anglers fishing resident trout or bass are often secretive about their methods. This may be justified in some instances because there are only so many fish available in the lake or stream and if the local expert tells too many people how to get them, there will be none left for himself.

Luckily, saltwater conditions are different. Sportsmen working

FRESH WATER

a run of salmon will take only a portion of the school. The migratory fish will move off in a short time anyway, so the expert loses nothing by helping others catch more fish.

SALT WATER

LURE COLOR

There is mounting evidence that fish can distinguish a wide variety of colors. We don't know very much about why they prefer one shade over another, but there seems little doubt that they can differentiate between even minor color differences.

Research experiments at Brown University showed that goldfish can be trained by color codes. The fish had to bump

126

colored targets with their noses to obtain food. They learned quickly to hit the proper target color, even when it was switched to a different position.

Fishing for salmon with bucktail flies requires the use of a wide

color selection for consistent success. Quite often, the coho will take only one color combination, completely ignoring all others. Bucktailers formerly relied exclusively on green and white or blue and grey flies for feeding coho (not in river mouth areas). Now, however, the color selection has widened considerably. A "hot" fly in recent years has been the "Fuddle-duddle" — a combination of purple and pink.

Experts have conflicting theories on which colors to use under different conditions. Bucktail expert Bruce Colegrave suggests light colored flies for dark days and dark colored flies for bright days. Hootchy-kootchy experts, on the other hand, find that light colors are best for sunny days and dark colors best on dark days. Freshwater bass experts tend to agree with the latter theory as their experience suggests bright colors for bright days and dark colors for dark days.

One of the few areas where there is general agreement is in matching lure color to the natural food in the area. This means green and white or blue and white in schools of herring or candlefish, or shades of pink in concentrations of certain types of shrimp.

However, we don't know how water color, reflection or depth

affect what the fish sees. What may look purple to us may look blue or black to a salmon underwater. Maybe this accounts for the success of reflective lures.

You can buy reflective tape for application to your own favorite

lure. And one local expert adds reflective tape to his Buzz-Bombs with considerable success. Maybe these reflecting lures which break white light into its component colors give salmon the flash of the color that it is seeking.

When we fish deep, we must concern ourselves with the fact that some portions of the color spectrum cannot penetrate very far under water.

DEPTH AFFECTS COLOR

Despite the scientific facts about the fade-out of colors at depth, commercial trollers off the west coast of Vancouver Island are discovering apparently contradictory information. In their continuing search for salmon, they are trolling deeper and deeper and moving out to the very edge of the continental shelf. They are finding large chinook at 600 feet or more. Even more surprising, these fish have definite color preferences.

At 600 feet there is no visible light of any kind. Yet the big chinooks can apparently distinguish color. It seems to defy all logic, but the commercial trollers insist that the salmon can choose between colors even at these great depths.

BECOME AN EXPERT

One of the best ways to become aware of the problems of the

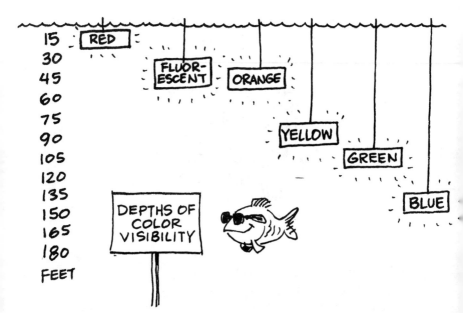

15
30
45
60
75
90
105
120
135
150
165
180
FEET

RED
FLUOR-ESCENT
ORANGE
YELLOW
GREEN
BLUE

DEPTHS OF COLOR VISIBILITY

average fisherman is to teach a night school class as I have done for the last several years. A few real beginners will enroll, but the vast majority are weekend anglers with a full set of tackle and a small boat. They feel frustrated at their lack of success and are very tired of the heckling from family and friends when they come home empty-handed. As one Spanish immigrant told me, "Many times I have gone for ze appointment with ze fish, but ze salmon never keeps ze appointment!"

Most students have never read any salmon fishing books, and those who have do not realize the importance of following the basic rules outlined therein. This really shows up when we go on field trips where *not one fisherman in 10 bothers to sharpen his hooks each time he starts out*. This omission alone probably costs him several salmon a season. (Several companies make hook-sharpeners, including my own firm, Charlie White Productions, P.O. Box 2003, Sidney, B.C. V8L 3S1 which sells the "Hook-sharp" for $12.95.)

CHECK LURE ACTION

Even more important is strict attention to the lure and its proper action in the water. Time and again the amateur strips out line without testing lure action beside the boat. This must be done each and every time a lure or bait is placed in the water. If the lure is not

working properly, you won't catch anything.

MOST DIFFICULT PROBLEM

Finding salmon is often the most difficult problem facing any fisherman, but particularly the weekender. There are many times when even the experts are skunked, but following a few common sense suggestions will increase your chances three or four-fold.

Instead of wandering aimlessly around the fishing grounds, you should have a definite fishing plan at all times. Keep your eyes and

ears open to what is happening around you. Look for seagull and diving bird activity, follow tidal currents and back-eddies, watch what successful anglers are doing and quiz them on lures, depth, and other pertinent facts.

My more diligent fishing students often call me several months after completing the course to report proudly on their successes. If they have absorbed the basic rules, they will have a new feeling of confidence when they go out for a day on the water.

However, most will also admit to some frustrating days when the fish just wouldn't bite or when other anglers caught fish and they didn't. "Now that I've pretty well mastered the basics," they will say, "how long will it take to become a real *expert*?"

"The rest of your life," is my reply. No one knows all the answers. This is what makes fishing the delightful sport it is.

KEEPING RECORDS

One of the best ways to become a proficient and more successful angler is to keep accurate records of each fish you catch.

Compiling your own personal catch data is really quite simple, but is probably the last good habit most anglers adopt. Not only does it seem anticlimactic to sit down and write-up your fishing results, it seems of little current value. Many anglers feel that they will *always* remember the details of today's catch.

Maintaining a fishing diary takes several years to pay off, but it provides an invaluable record of how, when, and where to catch salmon in your own favorite fishing holes. This is *exclusive* information available only to you... and available forever.

What information should be included? The migration habits of salmon and bait fish are extremely regular from year to year. They are likely to be found off the same points or drop-offs, at the same general depth, and feeding on the same size and color of lures as they were in previous years at the same time. You should also record information on the weather, stage of the tide, and the type of feed found in the fish's stomach.

LEE STRAIGHT

Lee Straight was outdoors editor of a daily newspaper for 33 years and is one of Canada's top outdoorsmen, an acknowledged authority on both tidal and non-tidal angling.

Lee is the author of another popular Special Interest Publication, "How to Catch Trout" and contributor to two other Special Interest angling books.

CHAPTER 13

MOOCHING

By Lee Straight

As fellow angler and author Charles White says in his basic text "How to Catch Salmon", there are no hard and fast rules about the sport. But one of the delights of the game is working up rules for yourself. The longer you fish, the more rules there are and the more "hard and fast" they appear to be. I have several such firm rules, and it distresses me to see other anglers ignore them, even as they no doubt frown when I seem to ignore one or more of theirs.

Would you believe that my first rule is to close-trim all knots? My friends say that this stems from my meticulous nature. I say it prevents tangles and reduces the amount of seaweed caught on my tackle. Mooching tackle is usually light and once you're accidentally hooked into a bundle of seaweed, it is much easier to tear hook, line and sinker through it if there are no tags on the knots.

When I mooch deep, I use shorter, thicker leaders. Winter fish, being smaller, allow lighter, eight-to-10-pound test leaders. Rambunctious summer coho require no less than 10-pound, while mature summer chinook call for no less than 15-pound. No heavier leader is required if you use light weights and limber rods, as they'll give with the action of the fish. But a fish soon pops thin leaders on stiff rods or heavy sinkers.

Mooching in tidal rapids with stiff, trolling rods has led to the use

of 30, even 40-pound-test leaders owing to the combination of resistant tackle, heavy current and bulky fish.

Short leaders, never more than five feet, prevent your bait (particularly a live bait) from twisting round and round the main

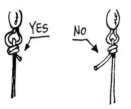

line as the sinker plummets when you're casting or just lowering your bait. When you can play it out carefully, moving the boat away as you do, or if you always cast it far to the side, then use a leader only a foot shorter than the rod; never longer than the rod as it makes netting the fish difficult.

MOOCHING SINKERS

The best sinkers for mooching are the crescent type. You may wish to cast some line and these don't tangle in midair. The best line in summer is stiff or hard nylon monofilament such as some of the French and German brands.

Average in stiffness are "Charterboat" and "Maxima Chameleon" (not the shiny green line). Stiff line lies more loosely in coils on the boat deck once the kinks are taken out of it.

Medium-stiff lines are better for winter stripcasting mooching as the lower temperatures make hard nylon more likely to kink. My favorite for winter mooching is a medium-limp line called "Stren" — either the "Super" (blue) or the "Golden" variety. They have very little "memory" or tendency to kink, are highly visible over the water or coiled at your feet, and tests have shown the fluorescent tint doesn't frighten fish.

STIFF LEADERS BEST

New brands of medium-stiff monofilament line are regularly marketed. I just don't trust discount-labelled, usually very limp monofilament line and confess that, after break-strength, I lean to dark brown tones of line. And I avoid shiny line more than brightly dyed line.

Most brands I like are quality lines at "quality" (high) prices. Certainly their excellent knot-strength indicates quality. They flat-

HM-M-M... .

ten out and weaken less readily in knot-tying and are less susceptible to crushing underfoot when stripcasting or mooching. Morever, they can take being nicked from flying hooks or from scrubbing on rocks, fish scales or fish teeth.

For leader material I favor the hardest, most neutral tinted monofilaments — hardness to resist nicking; paleness to fool the fish. A salmon gets a long steady look at a leader, mooched quietly far below, so you need all the camouflage you can get.

I use high-grade monofilament line for everything — leader, trolling lines, spinner and flycasting tippets.

The type of reel seems unimportant for mere mooching, but if you like to stripcast, then a single-action reel is preferable as the handles are less likely to catch loose loops of line when stripping it into the boat. Single-action reels also are, like fly reels, far more sporty for playing fish.

Some experts, desiring only to hide their good luck from eyes in nearby boats switch off the ratchet drags on their single-action reels, leaving just slight center-pin drag to keep the reel from running wild. They wish to hide the number of pulls of line they make as they lower their bait, even faking their hand movements. And they like to play fish in silence, even holding their rod-tips in the water as long as possible. The world's getting just too competitive. I like to let my reel howl as a strike, far below, proves to be a salmon and runs and runs, oh-boy-oh-boy!

HOOKS AND RODS

While all rods seem fine, there is a great advantage in long, limper-tipped rods for mooching. For one, their light tips react better to your own live bait or to the strikes of fish. Basically, when the tip is jigging, you don't snatch up the rod and strike. You wait until it takes a deep bow or goes suddenly straight.

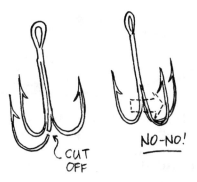

I use two treble hooks, tied well apart, for pure mooching. If I'm going to mix in some casting, then I like the front or top hook to be a single, just to reduce the chance of the two hooks fouling one another while sailing through the air.

I'm still undecided about actual hook size. Small, Number 10 or Number 8 trebles no doubt hook more reliably, but they also pull out quicker. I suspect they may be held by the fish longer since they aren't such a mouthful of metal. So I swing among sizes 6, 8 and 10, but I usually advise size 8.

Some anglers believe in pinching together two of the hooks, making a crude (and weakened) double based on the wild, unsubstantiated belief that the fish is less likely to throw the double hook. Suit yourself on that one. If you do remove one point of a treble, note that a third is always soldered to a double. Cut off that third

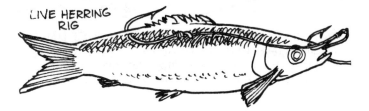

LIVE HERRING RIG

SINGLE HOOK RIG FOR MOOCHING WITH LIVE HERRING

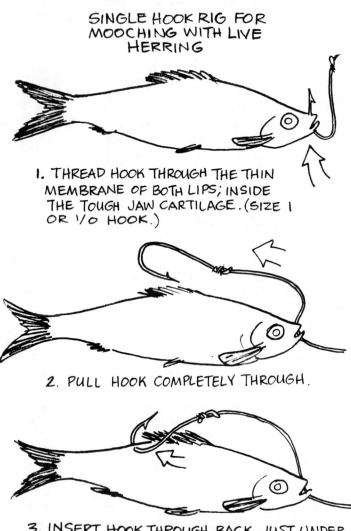

1. THREAD HOOK THROUGH THE THIN MEMBRANE OF BOTH LIPS; INSIDE THE TOUGH JAW CARTILAGE. (SIZE 1 OR 1/0 HOOK.)

2. PULL HOOK COMPLETELY THROUGH.

3. INSERT HOOK THROUGH BACK, JUST UNDER SKIN, BEHIND DORSAL FIN. BE CAREFUL NOT TO PUT HOOK TOO DEEP OR FISH WILL BE INJURED OR PARALYZED.

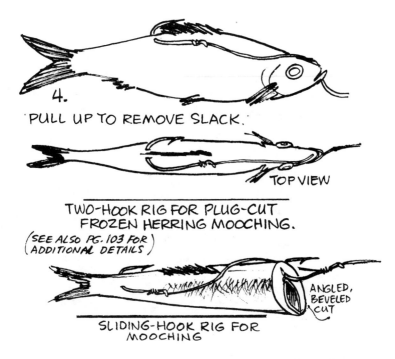

4.

'PULL UP TO REMOVE SLACK.'

TOP VIEW

TWO-HOOK RIG FOR PLUG-CUT
FROZEN HERRING MOOCHING.

(SEE ALSO PG. 103 FOR
ADDITIONAL DETAILS)

ANGLED,
BEVELED
CUT

SLIDING-HOOK RIG FOR
MOOCHING

with pliers, rather than pinching it against one of the others.

I like herring strips large in winter, small in summer, to match the prevalent size bait food. I cut them broad in winter, slender in summer, but with well shaved, sensitive tails. With live herring I always hook them in the nostrils and just back of the dorsal.

ROWBOATS STILL TOPS

Easily the best method of mooching is with a rowboat, just "mooching" along, as the name implies, keeping your lines down at an angle of roughly 45 degrees or halfway between vertical and horizontal, the rower watching his two rod-tips diligently. In mooching with a motor, speed of the boat is a problem. Few can hold it down enough to allow the lines to sink deep. Winter salmon are anywhere from 10 to 200 feet or deeper in full light and perhaps briefly near the surface at dawn and dusk. Great depth is a requirement and one of the advantages of mooching over trolling.

If you must use your more comfortable power boat in winter, then anchor. Or drift in the wind, take in your lines, motor back to the starting point, let down the lines and drift again. Some anglers will catch fish by power-mooching with heavy sinkers of six to

139

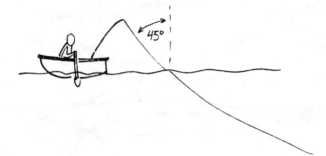

eight ounces in summer but seldom do so in winter. The lines just don't get down.

Here's an example of how one winter-time moocher deviates from the short leader and long rod technique. He uses a six to

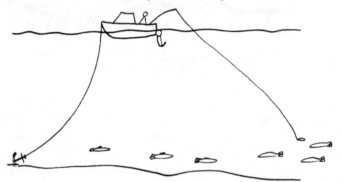

16-ounce slip-sinker, set just above a tiny swivel, joining the main-line to a 50 to 75-foot leader of no more than eight-pound test, and as light as — brace yourself — two-pound test. He plays the fish from a short but limber "trout" trolling rod and free-running reel, takes literally hours to let the fish tire, calmly and delicately removes the sinker when it comes close enough, then reels the small swivel through the rod-guides onto the reel drum. He has taken 20-pounders on two-pound-test that way.

GETTING STARTED

When starting, I nearly always let one line right to the sea bed, then quickly wind in 20 turns to keep it clear of the bottom fish that lurk down there. That is, unless I want a ling cod, in which case I tolerate many hookups with rockfish while trying to fish where lings are found (rocky reefs in fast tides, 60 to 200 feet deep).

Lings, by the way, are no pushover and almost *demand* light

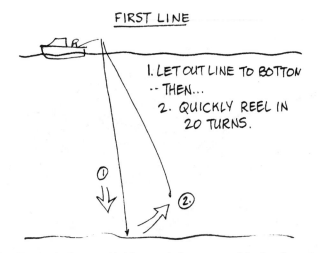

FIRST LINE

1. LET OUT LINE TO BOTTOM
·· THEN...
2. QUICKLY REEL IN
20 TURNS.

tackle. They do have prickly teeth but your thin leader usually stays between those teeth, not cutting. A dogfish, on the other hand, rasps its way through thin leaders. "Fish light for lings" is a rule of the sport. But just take your time.

The second and other lines I lower at intermediate distances below the boat, unless anglers already on the grounds tip me off to the likely depth. This experimenting with depths is essential and one of the reasons why moochers catch more salmon than trollers, once they know the area that salmon are favoring.

Now that we're fishing, we have long, delightfully quiet hours to

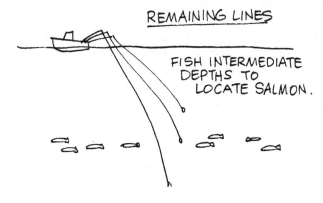

REMAINING LINES

FISH INTERMEDIATE
DEPTHS TO
LOCATE SALMON.

141

idle away, one of the pleasures of mooching versus trolling with a motor. Alertness, however, is the key to success, so it isn't as sedentary a sport as it appears. Sure, snooze off if you're anchored

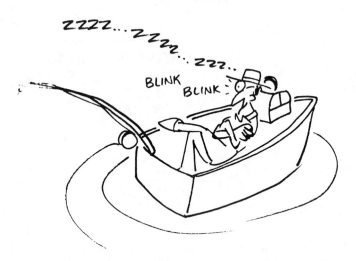

or tired, but when you do you're settling right there for maybe one third of the catch. Watching the rod-tip tells you whether or not the fish has finally tried to swallow the bait and lets you know when to strike home the hooks.

WHEN TO STRIKE

A salmon "munches" at a still bait, whether a strip bait or live herring, then grabs it and moves off, trying to swallow it. Your leader may block its attempt to do so or it may detect the hard hooks in the bait and in both cases spit out the bait. It is during this interval that the alert moocher has snatched up his rod and struck, impaling the fish. That's why it is particularly important to reel speedily when the rod-tip straightens, showing that even the weight of the sinker has been lifted. The salmon is heading toward the surface and you must work fast to strike it.

WHAT'S ON THE LINE?

In waters where "coarse" fish abound, it is difficult to tell immediately whether or not a fish is a salmon. But salmon, once well hooked, almost invariably move off fast, slanting the line outward at a speed never matched by rockfish or dogfish and only occasionally by ling cod. A bait struck, then dropped, showing

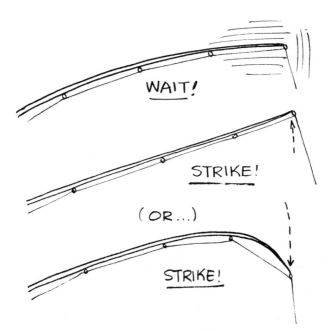

scratches or slashes has almost certainly been struck by a salmon. Ling cod, hake and rockfish also will slash a bait but more often just gulp it. If it's just scraped or is chopped clean, it likely was struck by a dogfish shark.

Once well into a fish and free of your anchor, don't be tempted to motor straight above the fish. They have more power that way,

something I learned from playing halibut and later proved to my satisfaction on heavy salmon. It is better to stay to one side,

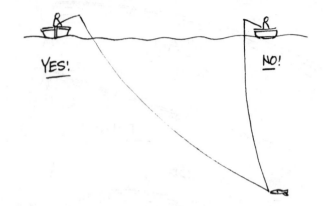

dragging them off course, so to speak. They tire much more quickly. If a fish sounds, then becomes immobile, it is almost certainly a ling cod. You must then keep pressure on it at a wide angle, circling. It probably has its nose under a rock.

Finally, a word of advice about guiding others, usually friends from afar who've never fished before. Or, worse, who have fished for small stuff that they're used to cranking right in.

Always, right at the start, lecture them politely and briefly about what to do when a fish strikes, letting the fish run all it likes. The

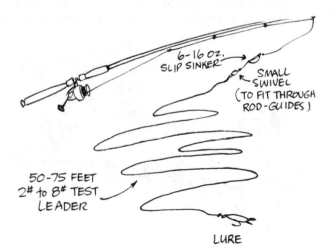

worst fault of beginners is freezing on reels, then popping those light leaders we must use for mooching. Tell them you've a mile of line on the reel, that even a whale couldn't take all in one run, then just say it's not a tug-of-war but a trading game. "The fish takes all the line it wants while you (the beginner) just keep your rod pointed to the sky and wind line back gently as the fish lets you. Rod high, no grabbing the reel to stop it whirling — but gentle control on the edge of it."

"Tight lines," tell them, "means a running fish, not a fish having his head torn loose."

TED PECK

Ted Peck is considered by many to be Western Canada's best known outdoor sportsman. From 1960 to 1966 he was the host of the popular weekly television show "Tides & Trails." He has introduced the Ted Peck line of fishing equipment, sold exclusively in all Woodwards, B.C. and Alberta stores.

He currently operates a charter fishing service from his 32-foot, custom-built Grenfell sportfishing cruiser, the Kelowna Kutie. *Over the years Ted has taught many thousands of novices to acquire both the skills and thrills of light tackle fishing for salmon.*

CHAPTER 14

CHINOOK AND COHO KNOW-HOW

By Ted Peck

The ensuing thoughts and reminiscences cover over 50 years of trial and error, success and failure, and many thousands of pleasant memories in the pursuit of two of the world's most magnificent game fish, the chinook and coho salmon.

Later I intend to go into some detail about methods, gear and best times to fish. But before that I feel strongly that a basic working knowledge of both species is paramount before one sets out to bring home a salmon dinner. I will deal with each species separately since, while there are many similarities in their histories, life patterns and habits, there are enough important differences that you should keep each one separate in your mind.

THE CHINOOK

First, then, let's take a look at the chinook or spring salmon. Its official, internationally recognized name is chinook, but equally popular are the following: Spring, used mainly in B.C. and derived from the fact that they are usually the first into their home rivers most years. From this name come also the names jackspring and winter spring. Other descriptive names are king, used extensively

in the U.S. and Tyee, the Coast Salish Indian name for chieftain or champion (designating individual specimens of over 30 pounds in weight). Quinnat is the named used in New Zealand where they have been successfully transplanted, and, finally, blackmouth is used extensively in Washington State to designate immature fish from four to 20 pounds caught in saltwater during late fall, winter and early spring.

As is the case with all five Pacific salmon species, the chinook belongs to the genus *Oncorhynchus* and the species *tschawytscha*. Oncorhyncus is a Greek word meaning "of the hook nose" and tschawytscha is a Russian name used as far back as 1792 on the Kamchatka Peninsula and in Alaska.

Chinook are by far the largest of our Pacific salmon with some individuals exceeding 100 pounds and up to five feet in length. The largest I have ever heard of was an Alaskan specimen weighing 135 pounds. The sport-caught record came from the Kitsumkalum River in B.C. and weighed 92 pounds.

Most chinook return to their native rivers to spawn and die in their fourth or fifth year, but individual races from certain rivers stay out at sea until their seventh or even eighth year and hence attain their tremendous size.

Others mature as early as their third year, at which time they ascend their spawning stream. These fish, invariably males of up to

eight or nine pounds, are known as jacksprings or simply jacks. The reason for the existence of the jack is that nature provides an excess of males in all salmon species, so that a portion of every race develops one or two years early so that no spawning female is left unattended if her mate has been killed en route to the river.

Depending on their individual race, and from which river system they originate, the young chinook salmon spend varying amounts of time in their native fresh water rivers and lakes. The time spent

before migrating to the ocean extends from 90 days (as is the case in most short Vancouver Island streams such as the Big Qualicum and Puntledge systems) to as long as two years in the case of such races as those originating far up the Fraser or Skeena systems. Typical two-year migrants could be found in the Stuart, Takla and Tembleur Lake chain in North Central B.C. These fish all end up at the mouth of the Fraser as six to eight-inch smolts.

Looking back through old statistics of commercial chinook salmon landings on the Columbia, Fraser and Skeena rivers, it can be shown that chinook salmon entered these river systems every month of the year. At least they did in those days, but today, with major pollution problems and many of the runs being vastly de-

A young fisherman displays a nice chinook taken driftfishing.

pleted and some even wiped out, it would still be fair to say they are available to the sport fishing public for longer periods of time, both in fresh and salt water, than any other species.

Another reason for the more or less constant availability of chinook is the resident stock of chinook known colloquially as "homesteaders." In the majority of instances most chinook salmon migrate far from their river of origin, some as far as 1,500 miles. However, these vast ocean migrations are not typical of all individuals in any given race. Percentages vary, of course, but it would be reasonable to guesstimate that somewhere in the neighborhood of eight to 15 per cent of young chinook in any river's race never migrate any distance at all from the mouth of that river. This is certainly true of the chinook salmon in many of the mainland inlets leading from Georgia Strait and on both the east and west coasts of Vancouver Island.

Another factor contributing to the availability of year-round chinook in southern B.C. is the pattern of consistent northward migration of many Columbia River and Washington State hatchery-raised chinook.

IDENTIFICATION AND FEEDING PATTERNS

Before we leave the chinook, here are some details on recognition and basic habits and feeding patterns. First, recognition: You are likely to encounter them in salt water at any size from a barely legal 18-inch grilse to a tyee in excess of 50 pounds. With the larger specimens over 20 pounds there is, of course, no doubt that you have caught a chinook, as no other species attains this weight, with the possible exception of a few chum and coho in northern waters.

As far as identification is concerned there are four easy ways to positively identify your catch as a chinook salmon:

• The spots appearing on the caudal (tail) fin appear on both lobes (halves), the upper and lower, and usually the silver sheen on the fish's side extends right out onto the tail as well.

• The inside of the mouth and gums are black (thus the name blackmouth) and filled with sharp conical teeth pointing backwards.

• The fish, in addition to having a heavily spotted back, has the longest anal fin of all salmon species found on both coasts of North America. This fin is found on the underside of the fish and is the one farthest back, closest to the tail; it will have 15 to 19 rays, or miniature divisions.

• Smell the fish. When taken from salt water all chinook salmon

give off a characteristic pungent, acid odor. This odor is not what you would call a "fishy" smell, but rather the typical aroma of a fresh-caught chinook. I have been taking blind people of all ages fishing now for over 37 years and it never ceases to amaze me how each one of them can identify, by smell, a recently caught chinook.

Now for the habits and feeding patterns of the chinook salmon. Chinook feed mainly on herring and other small fish such as anchovy, sand lance, smelt, stickleback and surf perch (shiner) —

depending on availability. They also feed upon squid and certain members of the shrimp family.

Habits and patterns vary from location to location, but as a general rule chinook salmon are both feeding and most active in salt water three times a day.

These times are from first light until 9 a.m.; the two hours when tide is at its lowest during the day; and again, at evening, during the last hour of daylight. Moreover, some places are traditionally most

productive during only one of the time periods mentioned above and are only so-so during the other two. It depends on the location.

One last thing you should know is the depth at which chinook swim at different times of day.

After many thousands of observations I have found the following depth situations to be reasonably reliable: Other than at first and last light, most chinook will feed in the bottom third of the water up to and including 250 feet. At dawn and dusk there will be a larger percentage of feeding chinook fairly close to the surface, but still most of them will be found from mid-water down.

THE COHO

The coho *(Oncorhynchus kisutch)* salmon has only one other name — the silver. It is called silver south of the 49th parallel and in Alaska. Some commercial canning and marketing organizations add the "e" to its name, giving us "cohoe," but for the most part, coho is the name most recognized in western Canada.

Like its bigger cousin the chinook, the coho is a beautiful, streamlined and well proportioned fish. Its salt water coloration is much the same as the chinook, being dark green on the back, bright silver on the sides, and pearly white on the belly. It has black spots on the back and on the top half of the tail. Its mouth and gums are predominantly white as opposed to the chinook's which are black. The coho does not possess an odor when first taken from salt water.

The size of coho salmon ranges from one to 30 pounds with mature adults often between six and 18 pounds.

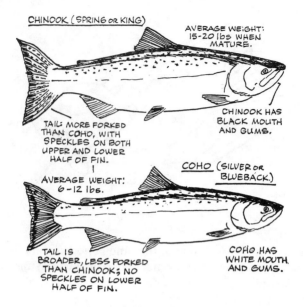

CHINOOK (SPRING OR KING)

AVERAGE WEIGHT: 15-20 lbs WHEN MATURE.

CHINOOK HAS BLACK MOUTH AND GUMS.

TAIL: MORE FORKED THAN COHO, WITH SPECKLES ON BOTH UPPER AND LOWER HALF OF FIN.

COHO (SILVER OR BLUEBACK.)

AVERAGE WEIGHT! 6-12 lbs.

TAIL IS BROADER, LESS FORKED THAN CHINOOK; NO SPECKLES ON LOWER HALF OF FIN.

COHO HAS WHITE MOUTH AND GUMS.

The world's record sport-caught coho was taken in Cowichan Bay by Patty (Mrs. Lee) Halberg in 1947. It weighed 32 pounds. Most of us will seldom encounter one over 16 pounds in southern B.C., but if you plan a trip to the Queen Charlotte Islands in September and early October, you stand an excellent chance of catching one over 20 pounds with some in the Copper and Tlell Rivers exceeding 25 pounds.

The coho was once native to all river systems in B.C., including some of the smallest of streams. Spawning in these minor watercourses is a common trait among many races of coho and may in fact be a reason for the species' downfall, especially with the encroachment of man as well as natural causes such as dry summers when these tiny creeks dry up. The coho's southern limit is the Sacramento River in California. It is also found on the other side of the Pacific in Japan and the Soviet Union.

I firmly believe that the world record noted above will be broken soon, not necessarily here in B.C., perhaps somewhere on one of the Great Lakes. The reason I say this is because of the phenomenally successful stocking programs currently underway on Lake Michigan, Lake Ontario, Lake Huron, and Lake Superior. Not long ago I saw a 21-pound coho taken off Thunder Bay, Ontario. Moreover, I have read fantastic news reports with photos showing coho over 20 pounds caught off the mouths of the Credit, Humber and Don rivers, all located near Toronto.

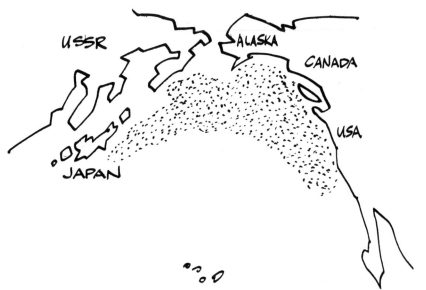

Unlike the chinook, the fully mature, spawning coho will only vary a few months one way or the other from a 3½-year cycle. Again, depending on the race, they spend six months to a year in fresh water and two to 2½ years in the ocean before heading back to the same tiny creek that hatched them. "Jack" (precocious male) coho are simply a year younger and reach sizes of 10 to 16 inches and weigh from three-quarters to 2½ pounds.

FAST GROWTH COMES LATE

An amazing feature of the coho is the unbelievably fast growth rate during its final six months of life. It takes a young coho well over two years to attain "grilse" size, but then come February of its last year and weight goes on at an amazing rate. A typical example would be two pounds in February, 4½ pounds in May, seven pounds in July, 12 pounds in mid-September and spawning in its home river in late November at 14½ pounds. A lot of this growth, of course, depends on feed availability in the ocean from May through October of each year.

During the month of May the young coho (known colloquially in B.C. as "bluebacks") switch from a primary diet of microscopic crustaceans to one consisting mainly of small herring, needlefish and sand lance. In years where there is a limited supply of young herring, there is a noticeable reduction in the average sized adult coho in late summer and early fall.

Something else that should be explained at this point is the fact

that there are two separate strains of coho available to us in Georgia Strait and adjacent inlets. I shall term them "resident" stocks and "ocean type" stocks.

The resident is the stock of coho that never leaves the inside waters of Georgia Strait. It provides us with most of our coho

fishing through the summer and early fall months. The ocean stocks travel great distances into the North Pacific at the grilse stage then return just prior to entering their spawning river. It's these that provide us with relatively few weeks and, in some years only days, of sport fishing opportunity in the ocean. These fish also bear the commonly used misnomer "northern" coho. I say misnomer because just as many of them re-enter local waters through Juan de Fuca Strait *to the south* as through Johnstone Strait from the north. When available, usually from mid-September on, their size is considerably larger than resident specimens, with individuals from 13 to 19 pounds being quite common. What percentage of each river's total run remains in Georgia Strait and what percen-

tage takes off for the open sea is not yet entirely known. A great deal of work in this field is now being done by the Department of Fisheries and Oceans.

There are two other large groups of coho now available to us which must not be overlooked. These are the hatchery stocks from both B.C. and Washington State.

The Department of Fisheries and Oceans is currently operating more than 20 hatcheries in B.C. and plans to develop more in the near future. Washington State operates over 50.

One other thing concerning coho is that in our waters they generally swim and feed in the top third of the total depth of water and are found usually within 30 feet of the surface. Finally, of the thousands of coho I have seen fighting on fishermen's rods, I have

never known one to last more than 15 minutes. The reason is that they kill themselves. They fight so hard, with so many runs, twists and pinwheels that the lactic acid build-up in their tissues fatigues them to the point of exhaustion in short order.

MOOCHING

Mooching is really little more than a highly refined form of good old still fishing with straight hook, line, sinker and natural bait. The natural bait is usually Pacific herring, as this is the bait most readily available to sportfishermen. Other bait fish may be used with equal and in some instances superior results, but you must catch it

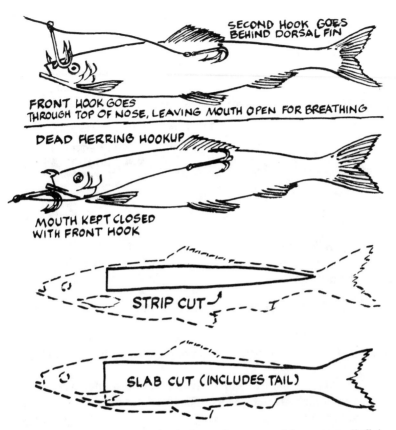

SECOND HOOK GOES BEHIND DORSAL FIN

FRONT HOOK GOES THROUGH TOP OF NOSE, LEAVING MOUTH OPEN FOR BREATHING

DEAD HERRING HOOKUP

MOUTH KEPT CLOSED WITH FRONT HOOK

STRIP CUT

SLAB CUT (INCLUDES TAIL)

yourself. Other bait may include anchovy, sand lance, needlefish and surf perch (shiners). All these will take both chinook and coho, especially when used live or fresh-killed the same day, but usually take considerable trouble to come by. I will therefore confine discussion on bait to the use and application of various forms of herring. These include live, fresh and frozen as well as strip, slab and plug-cut. These last three are available in frozen, prepackaged form in many areas, but you can save much expense by cutting them from whole herring you buy fresh or frozen in bulk.

Live herring is considered by many, including myself, to be the prime form of mooching bait. The following drawing illustrates how to hook up a live herring using an ideal sized specimen of four to size inches.

Hook size in mooching is entirely up to the individual and whether you use singles or trebles or whether you use one or two hooks, suit yourself. I have found that the use of two Eagle Claw #6, nickel-plated, 3X-strong trebles placed as shown in the illustration works best for me.

A bit on mooching gear now: Leaders should be at least three-quarters of the length of the rod which, incidentally, should be nine feet six inches to 12 feet six inches and possess a soft, limber tip.

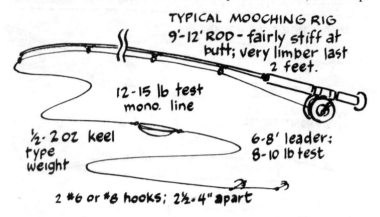

TYPICAL MOOCHING RIG
9'-12' ROD - fairly stiff at butt; very limber last 2 feet.

12-15 lb test mono. line

½-2 oz keel type weight

6-8' leader; 8-10 lb test

2 #6 or #8 hooks; 2½-4" apart

Weights vary from one-quarter ounce to six ounces, depending on tide flow in the area fished, with common sizes one, 1½ and two ounces.

Carry at least 400 yards of 11 to 18-pound-test line on any good four to 5½-inch diameter single-action center pin reel, and make sure that the leader you are using is at least two-pound-test less than your line.

It's worthwhile to note that the most successful moochers fish from eight to 12-foot car-top boats and rather than anchor, use their oars to hold the boat in position. This is not feasible, however, with larger craft and my personal recommendation is that all craft 15 feet and over should anchor when in confined areas.

BIG BAIT FOR BIG FISH

A lot of chinook are big fish, so don't be afraid to use big live herring (six to eight inches) when mooching. An excellent example of this was an accident which took place around mid to late June a few years ago. My wife and I were fishing in Active Pass with some good friends, Mr. and Mrs. Lloyd Stewart. As I remember, we had mooched three or four chinook salmon of about 15 to 25 pounds when we ran out of bait. We proceeded back to Herring Rock at the west end of the Pass to jig some more. Among the 30 to 40 herring we jigged my wife came up with a monster of 19 inches which most certainly weighed over two pounds and possibly almost three. It was the biggest herring any of us had ever seen. After heading back to the mooching grounds on the Mayne Island side of the Pass, we began fishing again, and strictly for a lark, I rigged the monster herring on bigger hooks and heavier weight and leader and started it on its way to the bottom to fetch up a big ling cod.

The herring and weight had not traveled more than 70 feet when the line went slack. I reeled back maybe 30 turns before I felt solid weight. I struck as hard as possible, felt it tug back then go slack again. By the time I had wound in the slack, my wife and I were staring dumbfounded into the face of the largest tyee I have ever seen. I can usually mentally "weigh" a salmon up to 45 pounds when it surfaces that close, but this one — no way. I can only guess at somewhere between 75 and 90 pounds. Anyway, it had swallowed the 19-inch herring and was certainly well hooked. But he took one look at us and the boat, pointed himself east-northeast out of the Pass and stripped my reel of 500-plus yards of line in under 60 seconds. We didn't have a chance, but as I say, don't be afraid to use big bait for big fish.

FALL FISHING

The advent of October marks the beginning of a period of prolonged change. A lot depends on weather. If the fall rains hold off, coho fishing continues at a brisk pace until the rivers fill up. Otherwise it's usually all over by Thanksgiving weekend. There is one exception, however, and this is the annual fall run of coho to the Cowichan and Koksilah Rivers at the head of Cowichan Bay. If

the run is on schedule, it usually enters the bay about October 5 and provides good sport by bucktailing and Buzz-Bombing into early November. Many large outside specimens are in this run, and remember, the world sport record was taken here (32 pounds). If the coho have entered their home rivers by mid-month, the lack of fish in many cases is made up by the appearance of the winter-feeding homesteader chinook.

WINTER CHINOOK AND CHUM

For the past 15 seasons, my boat has taken more winter chinook during November than in any other month. We fish exclusively by mooching in areas of Howe Sound. We use live herring if possible, but find fresh cut strips and slabs a close second choice. Many of the guests have taken hatchery raised chinook, so it follows that this program is working, on both sides of the border.

The second feature about November that I find most interesting is fishing for the annual chum salmon run in Cowichan Bay. The chum salmon, otherwise known as dog salmon or keta salmon (*Onchorhynchus keta*) is the last of the five Pacific salmon species to enter its home river. Neither the chum, sockeye, nor pink (humpback) salmon are legal game fish to be taken in fresh water, but all of them are quite legal in the sea. Indeed, many of each species are taken by accident each year by sport fishermen. Chum salmon fishing in Cowichan Bay, though, is no accident. It's done by Buzz-Bombing and can be a lot of fun. The fish range from 10 to 20 pounds and put up a creditable battle when hooked on light spinning tackle.

MIDWINTER'S EXCELLENT FISHING

The midwinter months of December, January, February and March are all excellent salmon fishing times, but so few people realize this fact that very little has been written about it. Weather, of course, plays a major role in determining when and where to fish. Keep in mind, however, that there are usually as many good days at this time of year as there are bad, and by wearing the appropriate clothes and making extensive fishing plans you can count on many comfortable, productive and rewarding days of salmon fishing in winter. The type of salmon available in winter is the resident "homesteader" chinook, usually weighing between four and 25 pounds.

VALUABLE TIPS

There are two especially valuable tips I have learned regarding salmon fishing in general, and light tackle salmon fishing in particular. One of the most valuable of these is how to recognize a typical chinook salmon strike and what to do during the ensuing 30 to 60 seconds.

In stripcasting and Buzz-Bombing the rod is invariably hand held and when you feel a hit you simply strike back hard to set the hook. In mooching, however, your rod will probably be in a holder and the method of detecting a strike is to watch the last six inches of your rod or rods with attention and devotion. Now, whereas coho

strike with ferocity, chinook *do not*. No matter if the fish weighs two pounds or 50 pounds, over 30 per cent of them mouth or play with the bait for a while before striking it from beneath. They then immediately begin heading for the surface as fast as they can swim. What you as the fisherman see is your rod tip straightening out and your line hanging limp and loose. To the neophyte moocher this appears as if his weight, bait and gear are resting on the bottom. And this could be the case if you have drifted into shallower water, but in all instances, treat this slack line and straight rod as the one thing you are looking for — the subtle hit of a chinook salmon. What you do during the next crucial half minute or so determines if you will catch the fish or not.

Here is what to do: Remove the rod from its holder, pointing the tip as low as possible, preferably right at water level. Begin reeling

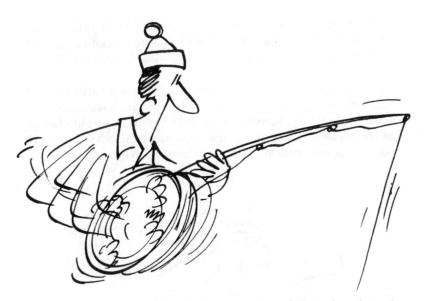

in as fast as you can until you feel some *solid* weight against the rod tip and it begins to bend back toward the water. When this happens the salmon has usually slowed down or stopped on his way to the surface, giving you an ideal opportunity to strike and strike *hard*. I

stress strike hard because of the distance from your rod down to the fish, and the stretch factor in nylon monofilament. Moreover, the flexibility of your rod also makes it necessary to drive the hook or hooks in sufficiently to hold. Make sure that you are holding onto the reel handles or the line somewhere between the reel drum and the first guide when you do.

LANDING NETS

Another good lesson I have learned over the years is the technique required in boating a salmon. When I was growing up salmon landing nets were somewhat of a rarity, as very few people could afford them and there were very few available on the market. Consequently most of us used some form of crude, handmade gaff hook.

A gaff in the hands of a long-time sportfisherman or commercial troller is one thing, but when an inexperienced sportfisherman gets hold of one, the results can be disastrous. Far too many good fish are lost right at the boat and a great many of them by people poking at thrashing salmon with a gaff. If you must use one, and they are cheaper than a good net, practise on ling cod and dogfish before you ever take a swipe at the only 30-pound chinook you're ever going to see close to your boat all season. And when you purchase a net, make sure it is two or three sizes bigger than you think you need, and at least two feet long in the handle. Modern, synthetic mesh landing nets are not that expensive and are worth their weight in diamonds at those crucial moments when a good-looking salmon is next to your boat.

Here are just a few hints on netting procedure. First make sure that the salmon is sufficiently played out before even putting the net in the water. It should be on its side, if not belly up. Next, show the fish the net by pushing it deep into the water in front of him. At this point, if the fish is not played out, it will take one last run. When you've got it back to the boat again lead the salmon over the mouth of the deep-sunk and slightly angled net bag. When about 60 per cent of the length of the salmon is over the mouth of the net, simply lift and lever the entire fish into it. The final stage is critical and should be done properly.

Now turn the net handle straight up to close the mouth of the net then lift net, fish and all up and over into the boat. Far too many 20 to 50 pound salmon are lost each year by people trying to scoop them into nets that were not designed to land fish any larger than a five pound trout.

NOTES

NOTES

NOTES

NOTES

More great reading designed to ensure your fishing success

All these books are available at your bookstore or sporting goods store — or you can order them directly from BC OUTDOORS on the convenient order form at the end of this book!

HOW TO CATCH SALMON — ADVANCED TECHNIQUES
by CHARLES WHITE & GUEST AUTHORS

The most comprehensive salmon fishing book available! Over 250 pages. crammed full of how-to-tips and easy-to-follow diagrams! Covers all popular salmon fishing methods: Downrigger Techniques; Mooching; Trolling with bait; Tricks with Spoons and Plugs; Tips for river mouth fishing; Catching giant Tyees; Winter Fishing; Secrets of Dodger and Flasher fishing; Buzz bombs. Deadly Dicks, Sneaks and other casting lures – AND MUCH MORE!

$5.95

HOW TO CATCH SALMON — BASIC FUNDAMENTALS
by CHARLES WHITE

The most popular salmon book ever written! Contains basic information on trolling patterns, rigging tackle, fisheries Dept. information on most productive lures, proper depths to fish, salmon habit patterns, how to play and net your fish, downriggers, where to find fish! This is the basic book on salmon fishing in the North Pacific and now has been expanded and updated to include the Great Lakes region as well.

$4.95

CHARLIE WHITE'S
FISHING SECRETS

Charlie shares more than a hundred of his special fishing secrets to help improve technique and increase your catch. No fisherman can pass this one up! Illustrated throughout with Nelson Dewey's distinctive cartoons and helpful diagrams.

$6.95

LIVING OFF THE SEA
by Charlie White

A comprehensive look at the bonanza of marine life in the North Pacific. Here are detailed techniques for locating and catching crabs, prawn, shrimp, sole, cod and other bottomfish, oysters, clams and more! And how to clean, fillet, shuck — in fact everything you need to know to enjoy the freshest and tastiest seafood in the world. Illustrated with black-and-white photographs and lots of helpful diagrams.

$6.95

HOW TO COOK YOUR CATCH
by JEAN CHALLENGER

A great companion for our "How-to-Catch" books! Tells how to cook on board a boat, at a cabin or campsite! Shortcuts in preparing seafood for cooking! Cleaning and filleting! Recipes and methods for preparing delicious meals using simple camp utensils! Special section on exotic seafoods! Illustrated

$2.95

HOW TO CATCH SHELLFISH
by CHARLES WHITE

How, when and where to find and catch many forms of tasty shellfish! Oysters, Clams, Shrimp, mussels, limpets. Easiest way to shuck oysters. Best equipment for clamming and shrimping! When not to eat certain shellfish! What to eat and what to discard! Easy ways to open and clean shellfish! How to outrace a razor clam. A delightful book chock-full of useful information! Illustrated. New

$3.95

HOW TO CATCH CRABS
by CAP'N CRABWELLE

Now in a seventh printing, with revisions that show latest crabbing techniques! Tells how to catch crabs with traps, scoops, rings! Where, when and how to set traps! Best baits! Detailed description and illustrations of a much easier method of cleaning, cooking and shelling the meat! A great book, crammed-full of all you need to know about How to Catch Crabs. Newly Expanded Edition!

$3.50

WHERE TO FIND SALMON — Vancouver Island
by ALEC MERRIMAN

Where to Find Salmon combines catch dates and locations of more than 75,000 salmon caught in the season-long "King Fisherman" contest, as well as on-the-spot research, first-hand reports, and "local knowledge". Plus — Detailed maps of the "hot spots", and easy-to-read charts! Know when (and where) the runs arrive in each area, and plan your fishing trips accordingly! Fishermen using the information in this book are finding that the big runs of Salmon are showing up right "on schedule" each year! **$4.95**

A CUTTHROAT COLLECTION

A guide to Understanding and Catching the Mysterious Trout

The Cutthroat is being restored to fishable quantities by the Salmonid Enhancement Program. Until now little has been written about this popular, but mysterious quarry. This collection fills the void. Noted experts, Bob Jones, Dave Stewart, David Elliott, Ron Nelson, John Massey, Ian Forbes and Karl Bruhn pool their knowledge and experience to unravel the mysteries surrounding this elusive fish and help you understand, conserve, catch and cook it.

Great reading for both fresh and saltwater fishermen.

$5.95

MAKE YOUR OWN FISHING TACKLE

by Bob Jones

Put your hands to work — save money and have fun! Learn how to make your own tackle with well-known expert Bob Jones. Sixteen information-packed chapters cover lures, spoons, spinners, wooden plugs, spinner baits, leadhead jigs, all kinds of molds — and more.

There are more than 150 photographs and illustrations to guide you. Plus tips on use and safety. Now you can equip your tackle box for pennies rather than dollars — so you'll be prepared to risk your tackle in snag-filled waters where you previously avoided — and where the fish are usually found!

Make Your Own Fishing Tackle — a small investment to make you a more successful angler!

$8.95

BOOK ORDER FORM
BOOK ORDER FORM
BOOK ORDER FORM

To: **BC Outdoors**
**202-1132 Hamilton Street,
Vancouver, B.C. V6B 2S2**

Please send me the following books:

HOW TO CATCH SALMON — Advanced Techniques	# 0085 _____	at $5.95 $_____
HOW TO CATCH SALMON — Basic Fundamentals	# 0086 _____	at $4.95 $_____
HOW TO CATCH STEELHEAD	# 0082 _____	at $2.95 $_____
HOW TO CATCH TROUT	# 0083 _____	at $3.95 $_____
HOW TO FISH WITH BUCKTAILS & HOOCHIES	# 0087 _____	at $2.95 $_____
HOW TO CATCH SHELLFISH	# 0090 _____	at $3.95 $_____
HOW TO CATCH CRABS	# 0091 _____	at $3.50 $_____
WHERE TO FIND SALMON	# 0084 _____	at $4.95 $_____
DRIFTFISHING TECHNIQUES	# 0088 _____	at $5.95 $_____
HOW TO CATCH BOTTOMFISH	# 0089 _____	at $2.95 $_____
HOW TO FISH WITH DODGERS & FLASHERS	# 0093 _____	at $2.95 $_____
A CUTTHROAT COLLECTION	# 0116 _____	at $5.95 $_____
MAKE YOUR OWN FISHING TACKLE — Volume I	# 0128 _____	at $8.95 $_____
CHARLIE WHITE'S 101 FISHING SECRETS	# 0141 _____	at $6.95 $_____
LIVING OFF THE SEA	# 0142 _____	at $6.95 $_____
HOW TO COOK YOUR CATCH	# 0095 _____	at $2.95 $_____
DISCOVER BARKERVILLE	# 0115 _____	at $6.95 $_____
BOWRON LAKES	# 0140 _____	at $7.95 $_____
	TOTAL PAGE 1	$_____

LOGGING ROAD TRAVEL
  — Volume I   # 0100 _____ at $5.95 $_____
PRINCE GEORGE BACKROADS # 0102 _____ at $4.95 $_____
OUTDOORS WITH
    ALEC MERRIMAN   # 0105 _____ at $3.95 $_____
EXPLORING BRITISH COLUMBIA
    WATERWAYS   # 0103 _____ at $4.95 $_____
OKANAGAN BACKROADS
  — Volume 1   # 0104 _____ at $3.95 $_____
LOWER MAINLAND BACKROADS
  — Volume 2 - Fraser Valley   # 0097 _____ at $4.95 $_____
  — Volume 3 - Hope to Clinton # 0098 _____ at $4.95 $_____
  — Volume 4 - Garibaldi Region # 0099 _____ at $4.95 $_____
BACKROADS EXPLORER   # 0143 _____ at $9.95 $_____
GREAT HUNTING ADVENTURES # 0139 _____ at $7.95 $_____
HOW TO HUNT DEER AND
    OTHER GAME   # 0106 _____ at $1.95 $_____
HOW TO SKI CROSS-COUNTRY # 0125 _____ at $5.95 $_____
HOW TO SKI TELEMARK   # 0124 _____ at $5.95 $_____
MARINE PARKS OF B.C.   # 0148 _____ at $16.95 $_____
        Sub Total $_____
        Postage and handling (up to 4 books
          50¢ per book, 5 or more 35¢ a book) $_____
              TOTAL $_____

☐ My cheque for $_____ is enclosed
☐ Visa   ☐ MasterCard

_____
CREDIT CARD NUMBER   EXPIRY DATE

_____
SIGNATURE

_____
NAME (PLEASE PRINT)

_____
ADDRESS

_____
CITY   PROVINCE   POSTAL CODE
ALL PRICES QUOTED ARE CURRENT AT TIME OF GOING TO PRESS.
HOWEVER, AS BOOKS ARE REPRINTED, PRICES MAY CHANGE.

DRIFTFISHING

By Jim Gilbert et al

First printing 1977
Second printing 1979
Revision 1985

Special Interest Publications
A Division of Maclean Hunter
#202 - 1132 Hamilton Street
Vancouver, British Columbia

Canadian Cataloguing in Publication Data

Gilbert, Jim, 1932—
  Driftfishing

  ISBN 0-88792-031-4 bd.
  ISBN 0-88792-011-X pa.

  1. Fishing. 2. Fishing lures. 3. Pacific
salmon fishing—British Columbia. I. Dewey,
Nelson. II. Title.
SH449.G54   799.1`2   C77-002082-8

Cover Design: Wardle & Associates
Cover Illustration: Gerry Apuada
Inside Design: Beach House Graphics
Printed and Bound in Canada: The Jasper Printing Group